THE KINGDOM

Belongs To Little Children

BARRY ADAMS

Father Heart
COMMUNICATIONS

The Kingdom Belongs To Little Children
by Barry Adams

Published by Father Heart Communications
Fatherheart.tv

BIBLE TRANSLATIONS QUOTED

Cover Design – Steve Adams / Barry Adams
Cover Photo Credit – Trout 55 / Getty Images

Printed Book Edition ISBN: 978-0-9950190-0-3

DEDICATION

This book is dedicated to three special people.

The first person is a man who God used to impart His love through a hug to show me what it means to be a little boy with a big Dad. Thank you Jack Winter for being a champion of our Papa's love to a generation.

The second person is my granddaughter Riley, who has taught me more about love in the first year of her little life than I could have ever experienced reading a thousand books. Thank you Riley for just being you!

The third person is our youngest daughter Candice, who has demonstrated a daily courage and trust in God that has amazed and overwhelmed our entire family in this past eighteen months.

ACKNOWLEDGEMENTS

There have been many people that have influenced me along the way on my journey home to love. Time and space would prevent me from adequately expressing my appreciation to all of those who have spoken into my life but I do want to specifically acknowledge a few people.

I especially want to thank Jack Winter and James Jordan for the huge role these two men have had in my life. From the moment that I first met them in June 1998, my life has not been the same.

I am thankful that both of these men freely shared the depths of the riches of their own lives and welcomed me into the amazing community of love they called Fatherheart Ministries.

1 Corinthians 4:15 tells us that we may have ten thousand teachers in Christ but we don't have many fathers. While there was never any structural intent to our friendship, both Jack and James modelled the Father to me in more ways than I could have hoped for. I feel very privileged and honored to have known them both.

I also want to thank Dorothy Winter for giving me her blessing to include quotes from her late husband Jack in this book and Denise Jordan for the rich revelation she has imparted to my wife and I over the years.

There have been many other champions that God has used to enrich my life and to every one of them, I want to express my heart felt gratitude. I so appreciate all of the mothers and fathers of the faith that have generously shared their lives so that their ceiling could be my floor.

Thanks also to Felicia Murrell for the amazing job she did in editing this project. I also want to thank my son Steve for helping with the cover design and my daughter Candice for her invaluable assistance in both formatting and editing the book.

And last but not least, thank you to my wife Anneliese for being with me on this amazing adventure. I couldn't have done this without your love and support. Papa has used you many, many times to create a safe place for me when I was feeling completely overwhelmed and undone. I love you more than words can say and I'm so glad that we are learning to grow down together in our Abba's love.

CONTENTS

FOREWARD

I have had the privilege of knowing Barry for thirteen years. I have stayed in his home, travelled with him and for the last five and a half years, we've done a weekly webcast together.

I love Barry's teaching, his illustrations, his funny stories and our mutual love of technology. But there is one characteristic which stands above all others. He lives out of the place of having a childlike heart more than anyone else I know.

He has a simplicity of faith that dares to trust the Father when most others would have given up. He exhibits a trust in His Heavenly Dad to provide and care for him and his family in a way some would call reckless. He is one of the most generous people I know and is happy to freely share the revelation that he has freely received.

Barry's new book, *The Kingdom Belongs To Little Children*, is written from his heart. Knowing him as I do, I can tell you there is no pretense here – this is how Barry lives his life.

Too many of us complicate things and make our faith a tangled mess of rules and regulations. Barry strips all this away and shows us what the life of a child of Almighty God can look like.

In a world filled with striving and performance, this book shows another and a better way. Barry practically illustrates time and time again what Jesus meant when He prayed to His Father that the mysteries of the Kingdom were hidden from the wise and revealed to little children.

Matthew 11:25-26
25 "I praise you, Father, Lord of heaven and earth, because you have hidden these things from the wise and learned, and revealed them to little children. 26 Yes, Father, for this is what you were pleased to do (NIV).

As you read this book with the eyes of your heart, you too can begin to see the secrets of the Kingdom that Jesus revealed so that you can be more like Him.

Through Barry's own story, he shows us the things, which are hidden from the wise and learned yet revealed to those with a childlike heart. It is my pleasure to recommend this book to you.

Mark Gyde
A Father To YOU
http://afathertoyou.com

PREFACE

In June 1998, I came into a revelation of God's love for me that literally turned my life upside down. For the first time in my twenty two years of being a Christian, I finally realized why Jesus died for me on a cross two thousand years ago.

It was so that I could come home to the love I had been looking for all my life. And that love was found in my Heavenly Father's embrace.

All of a sudden, my entire focus turned from trying to be a good servant to learning what it meant to be a son. And not just a son to anybody, but a son to Almighty God.

This revelation of sonship has transformed my understanding of maturity in a way that is counter culture to the world and often in the church. Instead of trying to grow up, I'm learning that the secret to Kingdom greatness is actually achieved when we learn to grow down.

If Jesus says the Kingdom belongs to little children, then there must be many tangible benefits of Kingdom living that only those with a childlike heart can truly appreciate.

Over the years, people have asked me how I practically live out this revelation of the Father's amazing love for me. This book is my simple answer.

I believe our Heavenly Father created each one of us with a brilliant, one-of-a-kind canvas and it is in the returning to the blank canvas that we all had as a little child, that our Father can begin the restoration process of everything He originally intended for our lives.

With each passing day, I am discovering hidden treasures that can only be grasped by those with a childlike heart. In this place of learning to be little, I am really starting to comprehend just how big the Kingdom is.

My hope and prayer is that you would join me there too!

In Father's love,

Barry Adams

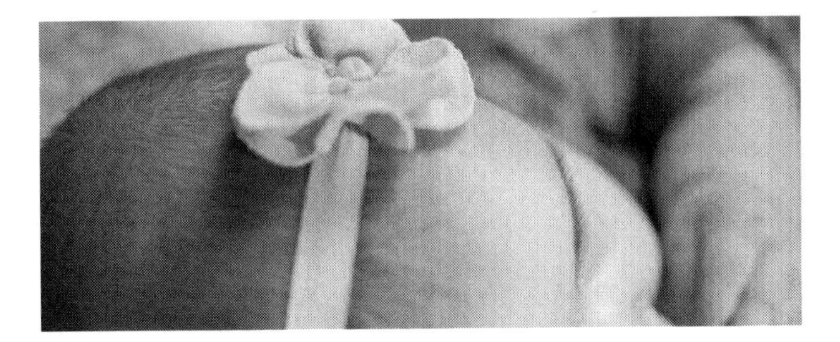

-1-
INTRODUCTION

We live in a society that teaches us to grow up as fast as we can so we can be independent, self-sufficient and a self-made success. Greatness is achieved through the acquisition of education, influence, money and power.

The more of a self-made man or woman you become, the more the world tends to celebrate your achievements. While all of this is well and good and does have some practical benefits, there seems to be another way that leads to true greatness in the Kingdom of God.

In Matthew 18, Jesus' disciples are arguing amongst themselves about who is the greatest in God's Kingdom. Maybe these were some of the questions they were asking… Will the most educated be the greatest? Will it be the most religious? How about the most disciplined? How does nobility factor into the equation? Who on earth will be crowned the greatest from God's perspective?

I love how Jesus responded to their bickering. He didn't give them a four-point sermon and He didn't try to argue with them. He simply called a little child to stand close to Him and said these words…

3 "Most certainly I tell you, unless you turn, and become as little children, you will in no way enter into the Kingdom of Heaven. 4 Whoever therefore humbles himself as this little child, the same is the greatest in the Kingdom of Heaven. 5 Whoever receives one such little child in my name receives me," (Matthew 18:3-5 WEB).

Can you imagine how this real life sermon illustration stopped the disciples right in their tracks? I am sure they were shocked to hear Jesus turn their understanding of the Kingdom's pecking order right on its head! After all, little children haven't grown up yet to be significant contributors to society.

They don't pay taxes. They don't earn an income. They aren't strong enough to care for themselves or others. And they don't have a developed intellect where they can reason for themselves. How on earth could God consider them to be more superior than the superstar leaders of society?

And yet, this is how the Kingdom works. It isn't the bold and the beautiful, but the weak and the small. Just in case Jesus' disciples didn't get what He was saying, He personalized it for them in verse 3 by saying, "Most certainly I tell you, unless you turn, and become as little children, you will in no way enter into the Kingdom of Heaven."

And so you have it. Unless we turn, repent and change, and become just like little children, we are going to miss all of the glorious benefits of Kingdom living. In evangelical circles, we would see this re-birth into God's Kingdom as the moment we are born again (John 3:3) and that would be true.

But in these same evangelical circles, many of us would make the basic assumption that while we enter the Kingdom of God as babes, we are expected to grow up as quickly as possible. After all, somebody has to 'get the job done' and little kids simply don't have the right stuff to make it happen.

It is this kind of mindset that fosters an unspoken environment of works-based Christianity where the goal is to become a competent contributor to the Body of Christ. Since little kids can't share the workload, their value only increases with their ability to produce.

I wholeheartedly agree that we are called to mature in our walk as we grow in the Spirit of Sonship (Galatians 4:6-7). But my question is…what is true spiritual maturity? If we use the world's system as the standard by which we measure, then greatness, strength, intellect and power would be the defining factors.

In this broken world system that we live in, maturity is measured through the grid of independence and self-sufficiency. Weakness is despised. The poor are abused and little children are often overlooked. However, if we see the Kingdom of God through a family paradigm, we will have to adjust our thinking.

If God is indeed 'Father' and we are His children, family rules take precedence over secular rules, corporate theories, organizational charts and power structures.

Until we realize that the kingdoms of this world are in direct opposition to the Kingdom of our God, we will miss the entire point of the Christian life. In our Papa's Kingdom, weakness overpowers strength and the foolish confound the wise.

Paul writes about what God values in 1 Corinthians 1:26-29:

26 For you see your calling, brothers, that not many are wise according to the flesh, not many mighty, and not many noble; 27 but God chose the foolish things of the world that he might put to shame those who are wise. God chose the weak things of the world, that he might put to shame the things that are strong; 28 and God chose the lowly things of the world, and the things that are despised, and the things that are not, that he might bring to nothing the things that are: 29 that no flesh should boast before God (WEB).

So why does God intentionally choose the foolish things of the world to confound the wise? Why does He validate the weak and the poor over those that the world considers at the top of the food chain? Wouldn't it make more sense that the rich, the wise and the strong would be a better reflection of the majesty and glory of God?

Well, not exactly. If you take a moment and just consider what got humanity's first couple into trouble in the first place, you will see sin's origins had its roots in independence (Genesis 3). Even though their intentions seemed noble enough (to be like God knowing good and evil), they were never created to live independent from the life flow of their Creator.

So if independence is not the biblical measure of maturity, what is? I believe Jesus summed it up best when He described His complete dependence on His Father in John 5:19-20:

19 Jesus therefore answered them, "Most certainly, I tell you, the Son can do nothing of himself, but what he sees the Father doing. For whatever things he does, these the Son also does likewise. 20 For the Father has affection for the Son, and shows him all things that he himself does. He will show him greater works than these, that you may marvel (WEB).

If the mature Son of God lived a completely dependent life on

His Dad, our definition of spiritual maturity has to be based on the same surrendered life that Jesus modelled here on earth. And if dependence is the measure of true spirituality, there is no better example of it than that of a little child.

Jack Winter used to say, "The smaller that we can become, the bigger that our Father can become on our behalf." Jack not only spoke of being "A little boy with a big Dad," he modelled it in his life. I can remember him telling me that we all have a choice in this life; we can choose to be small and enjoy all of the wonders of being loved by Almighty God, or we can choose to be big in our own eyes and miss the joy of being cared for by our Father.

Over the past seventeen plus years of walking in the revelation of the Father's love, I have tried to take Jack's words to heart in how I live my own life. This book is my attempt to express what I am learning as I become more and more comfortable with love.

I am so glad that I no longer have to try and 'grow up' to find the place of love and acceptance in God's sight. The life-changing truth of the gospel is that I am already loved and accepted! And it is in this simple place of believing that Almighty God is really my Dad that I have discovered 'growing down' is the real pathway to true greatness.

I pray as you read this book, your spiritual understanding will be awakened with childlike wonder (Ephesians 1:17-18). I pray you would find a new freedom to simply embrace your royal position as a little boy or girl with a really big Dad. No more, no less. For there is no greater honor God could bestow upon us than to call us His beloved kids.

1 John 3:1
See what great love the Father has lavished on us, that we should be called children of God! And that is what we are! The reason the world does not know us is that it did not know him (NIV).

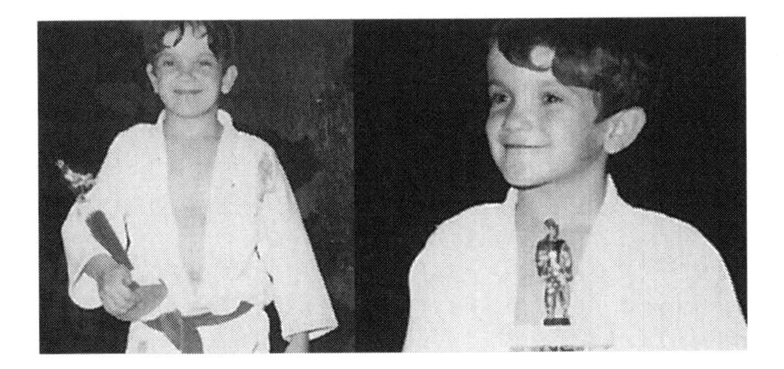

-2-
GROWING UP TOO FAST

In my generation, leaving home at an early age was considered a badge of honor. I started working full time at sixteen and left home at eighteen. Even among my peers, this was considered a pretty early start into adulthood.

When I look back at that time now, I realize this wasn't when I started to grow up. My ability to carry adult sized responsibilities started far earlier when I was just a little kid.

As early as I can remember, I always wanted my earthly dad's love and acceptance. While he never would have wanted me to feel this way, my entire focus as a little boy was to make him proud of me. My dad was a good father who did his absolute best to love me the way he knew how.

Considering he came from a broken home where he experienced rejection from his own mother, he did an amazing job. Yet, he was marked for life with the pain of not being loved the way he needed to be loved. Like all of us, he did what he could to cope.

My dad's daily dependence upon alcohol either masked or magnified his veiled anger. So as a little boy, I had to be very sensitive to his mood swings. I never experienced many spankings growing up, but in reality, I didn't have to. One angry look of disapproval from my dad could devastate my little heart. As a result, the fear of making my dad angry usually was enough to keep my behavior in check.

It was really important for me to gain my father's affirmation. I would feel his approval the most when I did something to earn it, like having a good report card. While this was not something that was ever spoken of in our home, I made the assumption that in order to receive love, I must continually do things to deserve it.

The most poignant example of my never-ending quest for love came on the judo mat. My dad was a blue belt in judo when he had to quit the sport as a result of an injury. In an effort to continue his passion for judo, he built a judo training center in our basement for my brother and I.

At seven years old, I started an intense training program that my dad created to prepare me to fight in weekend judo tournaments. I am sure my dad didn't make my brother and I work out every night, but as a little boy, it felt that way.

Every time I stepped on a judo mat to fight an opponent, my stomach was twisted in knots. And every time I lost a fight, I cried because I felt like I let my dad down. Unfortunately, my motivation to win was never rooted in the love for the sport but in the love for my dad.

The harsh reality was I couldn't emotionally afford to lose, and it was this motivation that caused both me and my brother to advance quickly in judo. By the time I reached eleven years of age, I was already a junior brown belt, which is the belt closest to black. This was the highest level a competitor under sixteen years of age could achieve in Canada.

Even though we gained a reputation for being top in our weight class, no number of trophies seemed to be enough. My brother and I kept on fighting as if we were looking for an elusive sense of affirmation that never came in the way we needed it to.

As I grew older, my unhealthy need to be affirmed through achievement accelerated in every area of my life. I skipped a grade, was voted the most popular student in my school and was even elected as president of the student council. I did everything I could to fill the hole in my soul but it never seemed enough.

My dad quit drinking after he was diagnosed with Cirrhosis of the liver when I was fourteen. In his time of sobriety, he announced to our family that he was going on a quest to find the truth. His journey started in the New Age realm and culminated with him receiving Christ after reading John 3:16.

My dad was a very prominent union leader and considered to be a tough cookie by his peers. He was never intimidated by bullies and was known to not back down from a fight if there was no other choice. His co-workers even nicknamed him 'Rocky' after a heavyweight prizefighter in the sixties called Rocky Marciano.

When my dad became a Christian, he had a complete change of heart. His colorful language and the ferocious way he negotiated with the management at the auto plant gave way to a gentler approach. The one thing that didn't change though, was his iron will conviction to lead and I am thankful it didn't.

As a result of his new found faith, he led his entire family to

Christ. My relationship with my dad dramatically changed after that but the lessons I learned on how love works didn't. I have heard it said that a child believes almost everything they are told in the first seven years of their life. If that is the case, what I learned in my early years was that love was conditional and something I continually had to strive to earn.

I graduated high school, bought my first car and began my nineteen-year career in the newspaper business at sixteen years of age. As a result of my drivenness, I experienced a measure of success in both business and church life.

During my business career, I was promoted seven times and received the highest individual award for sales excellence for newspaper advertising in Canada. At the same time, I was serving in a variety of leadership roles in my local church.

Needless to say, my professional and ministry responsibilities kept me quite busy in addition to raising three young children with my dear wife. Even though I was doing everything I thought I should do in life, no matter how much I accomplished, I couldn't find lasting peace. It was as if there was a 24/7 performance flywheel in the core of my being that I could never shut off.

Although I had the right theology of God's love, the tangible benefits of *living loved* seemed to elude me. My continual quest for affirmation kept me chasing things that would never bring lasting peace and rest.

It was in this season in my life that my home church invited me to come on staff as a full time associate pastor without me having to go to Bible school. I quickly agreed because I had hoped becoming a pastor might sort out my performance issues. I couldn't have been more wrong about that assumption!

I went from having one boss in the newspaper business to having over three hundred bosses in my church! I went from having definable, achievable goals in newspaper advertising to the intangible, never ending demands that seemed to be weighing on me as I worked in God's Kingdom. Needless to say, my need to perform didn't decrease. It went off the charts!

Desperate for help, I went to a 'Catch The Fire' conference in Toronto in October 1997 with the hopes that I could find answers to my many questions. There was an invitation for pastors to receive special prayer at one of the meetings. I ran to the front with great expectations. I had faith to believe God would do something for me if one of the conference speakers prayed for me.

One by one, every one of the speakers seemed to pray for everybody else but me. As my faith level fell, a young man came up to me, put his hand on my shoulder and said the following words, "I have a picture. You are a baby in your mother's womb and God is your Father, and right now He is reattaching your umbilical cord to Himself."

I didn't feel a thing. And to be quite honest, I felt a little disappointed that one of the main speakers didn't pray for me. But I wanted to be gracious, so I thanked the young man for praying and made my way back to my seat.

Though I didn't think anything significant happened, something awakened inside of me that I wasn't aware of until that moment. As I sat back down in my chair, I realized for the first time in my life what I had been tirelessly searching for. I was looking for the love of the Father my entire life. While I didn't encounter a tangible sense of His love that day, this is when I turned my heart towards home.

In hindsight, I think the reason I greatly value a childlike heart now is because I didn't experience it when I was little. When I should have been out playing and having the time of my life, I was instead living a very grown up life, carrying the weight of the world on my shoulders.

Instead of enjoying life as a little kid, I tirelessly worked to hear the words that would set my heart at rest and validate who I really was. Unfortunately, those words were never expressed in the way I needed them.

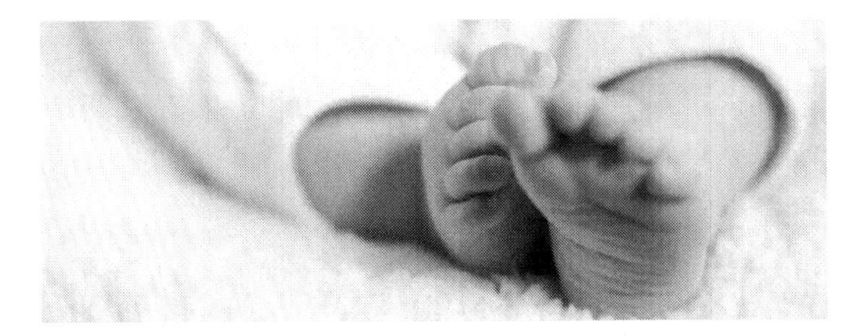

-3-
COMING HOME TO LOVE

After I came to the realization of what I had been looking for all my life, I was able to put some real form to my greatest need. I had a 'father hunger' and that hunger became more and more intense. I went to every meeting I could that had to do with knowing God as Father. I read every book I could possibly read on the Fatherheart of God.

Then, in November 1997, I attended a Father Loves You conference at Toronto Airport Christian Fellowship where a man named Jack Winter was speaking. He talked about knowing God as a Father in a way I had never heard before. At the end of one of his sessions, he invited a young lady onstage to demonstrate how he prayed for people.

Jack asked the girl about her relationship with her natural father and she broke down crying in front of the thousands of people in attendance. Jack tenderly ministered to her and asked if she could be a little girl who needed to be loved.

After she tearfully said *yes*, Jack invited her to hug him like she'd hug a father. Then he prayed this prayer as she embraced him, "Father, let my arms become your arms for your daughter because she has never known a father like you." I was standing at the back of the auditorium in awe as I watched Jack tenderly minister to this young girl. I wished Jack would do that for me too but with thousands of people in attendance, I knew that was impossible.

My 'Father hunger' continued for the next seven months until I found myself invited to a men's retreat in North Bay, Ontario with this same man, Jack Winter. I got the privilege of riding up to the conference with Jack and another man, James Jordan. I can remember stopping for lunch and being blown away by the way they talked about their relationship with their 'Father'. My hunger only increased.

The first night of the retreat, Jack spoke about the many misconceptions we place on God's fatherhood that are based on our own broken father relationships. For the first time, I realized I had been placing all of the same assumptions about God's fathering as I had experienced with my own father.

With my earthly dad, I was trying to win enough judo tournaments to win his love. With my Heavenly Dad, I was doing the same thing but used my church work as the means to try to win His approval. Needless to say, I was shocked to see I was treating God the same way.

That night, God dismantled my many misconceptions of His true nature. Through this new revelation, I was able to open my heart to see God as He was and not through my distorted perception of what He must be like if He is a father.

The next morning, James Jordan shared a two part message on how our relationship with our fathers can affect our relationship with Father God. In his first teaching, James shared how important it is to forgive our fathers for not being the fathers we needed. He likened forgiveness to cancelling a debt and used the parable Jesus shared in Matthew 18:21-35.

It was during this teaching I realized that even though I had forgiven my father on one level, there were much deeper levels of pain I had yet to forgive him for. I realized forgiveness was a process and not a once and for all decision I made when I first forgave my dad. This revelation gave me the permission to open my heart to forgive my dad for all of the areas he wasn't able to father me like I needed.

The second part of James' teaching that morning was on the Spirit of Sonship from Galatians 4:6-7. It had never occurred to me before that I had a responsibility in the relationship with my earthly father to have the heart of a son towards him.

When I heard that Jesus had a son's heart not only to His Heavenly Father, but also to His earthly parents, Mary and Joseph, I realized this was something I needed to deal with. It was then I became aware that at some point in my life, I had stopped having the heart of a son towards my own father. So that morning, God gave me the grace to repent of every judgment I had made towards my dad.

Jack wanted to demonstrate how he prayed for someone to receive the love of the Father at the final evening meeting. My friend, Dennis, who organized the men's retreat, asked me if I would be willing to be Jack's 'guinea pig'. I'd forgotten that seven months earlier, I wished Jack would pray for me. I'm glad God didn't forget.

Now I found myself at the front of the room facing all of these strangers and Jack turns to me and asks this one question, "Barry, tell me about your relationship with your dad." At that moment, a very painful memory came to the surface of something I thought I had forgiven my dad for.

Right then and there, I went from being a thirty-seven year old man with all his faculties in place to being a five year old, broken hearted little boy. I wept uncontrollably as I became more aware of the pain I experienced in my life long pursuit of searching for love in all of the wrong places.

Jack asked if I could forgive my father for not being the father I needed and I answered *yes*. He asked if I could forgive myself for rejecting my dad and I answered *yes*. And then he asked, "Barry, can you be a little boy that needs to be loved?"

At that moment, feeling the weight of the disappointment of not being loved like I needed, I didn't have to try to be a little boy. I WAS a little boy that needed to be loved and said a resounding, "YES!"

Jack invited me to wrap my arms around his neck like I would hug a father, which I did immediately. He then prayed the simple prayer that I heard him pray seven months earlier, "Father, make my arms your arms for your son because he has never known a father like you."

The only way I can explain what happened next is to say I felt wave upon wave of liquid love fill my soul. And I can honestly say it didn't feel like it was Jack hugging me. For the first time in my life, I felt like I was in the loving embrace of my Heavenly Dad!

Words fail to describe what that hug did for me. Being loved unconditionally and accepted by my true Father was like a healing salve to every broken part of my being. It was like God's love was touching and healing every area of 'un-love' that had scarred my emotional make up.

As a little boy who had tirelessly searched for love through the relentless pursuit of achievement, it was the best news ever to hear Father speak these words to my heart, “Barry, I don’t love you because you do anything to deserve it. I love you because you breathe.”

After my ministry time was over, I told Jack that for the first time in my Christian life, I finally realized what I had been created for. I had been created to be a son to my Heavenly Dad! For the first time in my twenty-two years as a Christian, I saw why Jesus died for me. He exchanged His life for my life so His Father could become my Father!

It was kind of funny because Jack used to travel with a dishtowel that he would put on his shoulder before hugging someone. Think of how a mother puts a towel on her shoulder before she burps her baby and you will get the picture. The only thing is, I hugged Jack before he could put the towel in place. Of course with all my tears and other stuff, I think I ruined his shirt.

This revelation of knowing God as Father has changed everything for me. It is like everything I thought I knew about the Christian life has been turned right side up. No longer do I see my relationship with God as something I have to strive to achieve and keep. I am loved completely and unconditionally by the source of love itself.

It is in this place of learning to rest in the eternal affection my Dad has for me, that being little really makes sense. I no longer have to try to be competent, powerful, or independent in His sight. I am free to be who He made me to be, warts and all!

My prayer is that you would know just how much your Heavenly Father loves you too. I pray that His love for you would consume every ounce of unbelief and mistrust that has been sown into you by a broken, orphan world system.

You were created to be a beloved child of Almighty God! This is your birthright and your God intended destiny. May you have the grace to settle into your new identity and find rest in His love.

-4-
TURNING MY HEART TOWARDS MY DAD

After coming into this deeper revelation of God's love for me, I realized I needed to ask my earthly father for forgiveness for not being a son to him. I thought the Lord would give me six weeks or so to work up the courage to approach my dad about this, but lo and behold, three days after the conference was the day.

It happened after a family dinner at my parents' house when my dad and I were still sitting at the supper table alone. He knew I had gone to some 'father conference' on the weekend and asked me how it went. When my heart pounded and my pulse raced, I knew this was the time to ask for my dad's forgiveness.

So I just blurted it out to him, "Dad, at some point, I stopped being a son to you and I just want to let you know that I am really sorry about that. Would you forgive me?" With his eyes filled with tears, he said, "Of course I forgive you." Dad then called the entire family into the dining room and said, "Barry's got something to tell you."

At that moment, I knew he wasn't trying to put me on the spot in front of the rest of the family. He was just excited that my heart turned towards him again. He wanted the rest of the family to hear it as well. When I left my parent's house that day, my dad initiated a hug to me, which was quite unusual. I don't remember experiencing many hugs growing up so this was very special for both of us.

A few months later, our home church hosted its first Fatherheart Conference with James and Denise Jordan. James encouraged me to be on the prayer ministry team despite my protests of feeling completely unable to impart the Father's love to others.

When I told James I wasn't qualified to impart God's love to others, he wholeheartedly agreed. Then he reminded me that it was God's Spirit that did the work, not me. Since I couldn't argue with that logic, I relented and became part of the ministry team.

I will never forget when I saw my earthly dad in the crowd responding to the invitation to receive ministry. I could see that he was looking for me as he came forward. We locked eyes and he found his way over to me and asked if I could minister the Father's love to him.

That moment was one of the most special times of my life. Knowing my dad's own story, how his mother rejected him and how he struggled with his relationship with his father, it was very humbling for me. So I asked him, "Can you be a little boy that needs to be loved?" and my dad said, "Yes."

I asked him to wrap his arms around my neck like he would hug a father and simply repeated the prayer I heard Jack pray, "Father, would you make my arms your arms for your son because he has never known a father like you." Love came to my dad that day in a deeper way than he had ever known before. I was deeply honored my Abba would allow me to be a part of my own dad's homecoming.

The next eighteen months were all about me learning to be a son, a son to my earthly father and a son to my Heavenly Father. Since having the heart of a son was new to me, I had lots to learn.

A year later, my dad contracted a very serious illness that even the specialists couldn't diagnose. Since he wasn't able to do some of the household chores he once did, I tried to help out the best I could.

I can remember as a teenager being forced to cut the grass and I didn't have a very good attitude about it. Now, as I was learning to have the heart of a son to my dad, things were different. Every time I cut the grass for him, I felt like I was not only honoring my dad, but I was honoring my Heavenly Father as well.

My dad's health declined to the point where he had to have emergency surgery in order to remove his spleen. Knowing he had less than a fifty percent chance of surviving the surgery, I wanted to visit him the day before the operation. As I was preparing to go to the hospital, I felt the Lord tell me to read Genesis 49.

I hadn't known why, but I turned to it only to discover that this was the account of Israel's last day on earth before he died. He had called all of his sons to him on this final day to bless each one of them. It was then I heard God say to me, "Ask for your father's blessing today."

I wasn't sure how to ask, but I did realize it was really important for me to do. So, at the right time when my dad and

I were alone, I went for it. I told him how much I loved him and how proud I was that he was my dad. I said to him, "Dad, would you bless me?"

He looked at me and said, "That's a good idea! I never thought of that." He put his weak hand on my head and recited prayers of blessings over me, my family and the ministry that we were entrusted with. It was both overwhelming and humbling to receive what I now see was a generational end of life blessing from my father.

My dad did survive the surgery, but his internal organs began to shut down. As a result, they transferred him to palliative care. After a couple of days in a comatose state, I asked one of the nurses why my dad was not passing. She said sometimes people hang on as long as they can if they are concerned about something. She also said even though my dad was non responsive, I needed to be careful of what I said around him because his hearing would be the last thing to go.

I asked the Lord why my dad was still hanging on and I felt the Lord say to me that he was concerned about my mom's care. So when no one else was in the room, I went really close to my dad's face and told him he didn't need to worry about mom. He had raised two good sons who would look after her the rest of her life. I told my dad he could go home now.

I may have been imagining it, but to the best of my recollection, I thought I saw a tear in his open eyes and I left the room. Within fifteen minutes or so, we were called back into the room as my father entered into the final stage of dying.

All of our family was gathered around my dad's bed and one by one, we all prayed prayers of blessing over him as we said our goodbyes. I was the last one to pray and the final words I said in my prayer were, "Father, into your hands do we commit our dad and your son. Take him home." At that moment, my dad breathed his last breath.

I was teaching a weekly Fatherheart course one night a week at a nearby church and I made the commitment to the Lord that I would still teach the class if my dad passed away as long as the funeral wasn't on the same day. My dad went to glory on a Friday and we had his funeral service on the following Monday. Tuesday night was the weekly Fatherheart class at the church.

Since all of the topics were already scheduled for the entire course, I spoke on the message that was planned for that night. To honor my father, I kept a photo of him that we used at his funeral projected on the overhead screen throughout my entire teaching.

I believe it was only the grace of God that got me through that night as I shared the pre-determined topic of *The Spirit of Sonship*. This was one of my favorite teachings because it was very personal to me. In this teaching, I talked about my own journey of learning to be a son not only to my Heavenly Father but to my earthly father as well. Having just said goodbye to my dad the day before made this evening that much more impactful for me and for the students.

My life is a living example of a little boy who was so transformed by the love of the Father that it changed my ability to be a son to my earthly dad. Because I experienced love that came directly from the source of all love, I received a healing in my heart that freed me from every unhealthy tie to my father.

The healing that I received from the Father gave me the ability to release my dad from every expectation of how he could father me. Instead of focusing on how he should have fathered me, my focus now became on how I could be a son to him.

I believe this is what the last prophetic word from the Old Testament is referring to when it points to the New Covenant. Jesus became the way for us to know that our Father's heart is turned towards us so that our hearts could be turned towards Him.

Malachi 4:5-6
5 Behold, I will send you Elijah the prophet before the great and terrible day of Yahweh comes. 6 He will turn the hearts of the fathers to the children, and the hearts of the children to their fathers, lest I come and strike the earth with a curse" (WEB).

-5-
THE BIBLICAL REVELATION OF FATHER

When I came into the revelation that Almighty God was really my Dad (2 Corinthians 6:18), it was like I put on brand new glasses for the first time. All of the Scriptures from Genesis to Revelation that spoke of God's Fatherheart for the world jumped off the page at me.

I have always had a deep appreciation for the Word of God but now in light of my Father's affection for me, many of these familiar verses had a much more personal meaning to me. For the first time, I really understood what Jesus meant when He said He was the way to the Father (John 14:6).

It still amazes me how this revelation of the Father's love can be veiled from so many. Though there are hundreds of descriptions of God's character in the Old Testament (Jehovah, El Shaddai, Elohim, Adonai, etc.), Jesus reveals God through one name in the New Testament. And that name is Father.

Not only did Jesus call God His Father, His life was a mirror image of His Father. Hebrews 1:3 describes Jesus as the "exact representation of His being" and Colossians 1:15 says that Jesus is "the image of the invisible God."

In John 14 when Jesus is having a discussion with His disciples about His soon departure, Philip asks Jesus to "Show us the Father and it will be enough." Jesus responds in verse 9:

Jesus said to him, "Have I been with you such a long time, and do you not know me, Philip? He who has seen me has seen the Father. How do you say, 'Show us the Father?' (WEB).

In a nutshell, Jesus was telling His friends that everything He did was a mirror image of His Heavenly Dad. Every baby that Jesus blessed was in fact, His Father blessing the baby through Him. Every sick person that Jesus healed was the Father expressing His life through His beloved Son.

Jesus introduced His Father into every situation He encountered. When the woman who was caught in adultery was humiliated and ready to be stoned, it was Jesus who brought the heart of the Father into the very center of that scandalous situation. Though Jesus spoke the words, it was His Father's ferocious love that protected a daughter whom religion sought to kill.

Even when Jesus washed His disciples' feet in John 13, He was only doing what He saw His Father doing. In light of the loving relationship the Father has with the Son, it only stands to reason that only the perfect Son could bring a revelation to the world of the perfect Father.

Hebrews 1:1-2
1 God, having in the past spoken to the fathers through the prophets at many times and in various ways, 2 has at the end of these days spoken to us by his Son, whom he appointed heir of all things, through whom also he made the worlds (WEB).

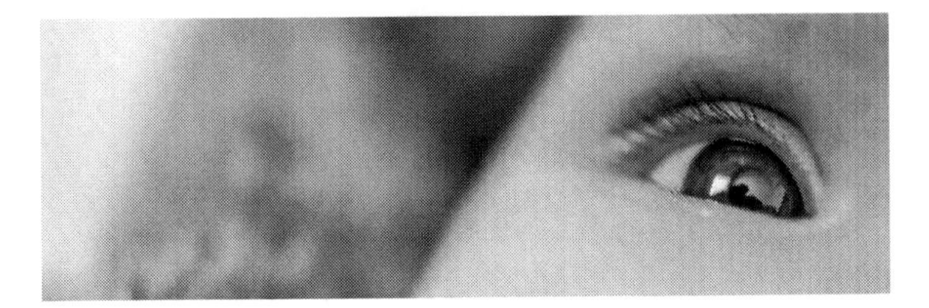

-6-
THE CREATION OF FATHER'S LOVE LETTER

It was the biblical revelation of God's Fatherheart that overwhelmed me after returning home from the men's retreat aforementioned. From Genesis to Revelation, it was like I was seeing God's heart for His kids everywhere I looked.

One day in prayer, I asked Papa to help me bring some of these Bible passages into one stream of thought. In my heart, I heard Him say, "If you put them in the right order, they will form a love letter from me to the world."

In December 1998, I prepared a sermon illustration where I organized and paraphrased some of these much loved Scriptures. It wasn't long until I had assembled a selection of these paraphrased passages and they did indeed take on the form of a love letter.

I was getting this slide presentation ready to show at the end of a message I was going to share in January 1999 on knowing God as Father. I added Brian Doerksen's song, 'Faithful Father' as the music soundtrack and called my sermon illustration ***Father's Love Letter***.

I was really surprised at the impact this eight-minute video had on the people in our congregation. Many were weeping as they read each line. Since it affected our home church so much, I thought it might be helpful to share it online with others.

So in November 1999, we launched a new website called FathersLoveLetter.com with very little fanfare. My friend, Ron, helped me build a website to host this single streaming flash video file.

In January 2000, we received a panicked phone call from our Internet service provider telling us that their web server was in jeopardy of crashing because of our website. Apparently, there were so many people on our website watching the Father's Love Letter video, that we were taking up all of their available bandwidth!

They gave us twenty-four hours to reduce the file size of the streaming video or they were going to shut us down. We were truly surprised to hear that there was so much interest in this one video and we made the necessary changes to keep our website live.

In 2001, a friend of mine suggested that we should have a narrated version of the Father's Love Letter produced because he had difficulty reading the text on the slides. It wasn't long after he suggested this, that a man named Roy Lamont, contacted us and offered to provide a narration version if we wanted it.

Never in our wildest dreams could we have imagined just how perfect Roy's voice was for the narration. Not only did he have an amazing fatherly voice, but he had a fatherly heart as well. My friend, Robert Critchley, produced a music soundtrack to compliment Roy's narration and before we knew it, we had a new version of the Father's Love Letter that we still use today.

The only language that we intentionally translated the Father's Love Letter into was German because that was my mother-in-law's first language. Every time she read the English version, she cried because she was given up for adoption at five years old. It was our desire to have her hear the Father calling her home in her mother tongue so we had the letter translated by a friend of ours.

Once we added the German version of Father's Love Letter onto our website, the floodgates opened with people from around the world asking that the Father's Love Letter be translated into their language too. To date, there are over one hundred language translations on our website and I'm sure there are even more languages translated that we don't know about!

Over the years, millions of people have visited our site and we have heard thousands of stories of how God has transformed people's lives by revealing to them that He is their true Father.

The Father's Love Letter has been broadcast worldwide on television and radio, appeared as full page newspaper ads and has even been delivered door to door in entire nations.

Right from the beginning, I felt the Lord say to "Do it for the one." I am so glad that we have always been focused on 'the one' because in reality, every person who comes home to the Father gets their own party (Luke 15:7).

Time and space would prevent me from sharing the many stories I have heard throughout the years. I am so thankful for every person who has shared this letter with another person. As far as I am concerned, they are the true heroes.

The Father's Love Letter has been shared in jungles, schools, prisons, drug rehab centers, group homes, pregnancy crisis centers, on the streets, in strip clubs, in churches, and in pretty much every other place you could think of. It has brought comfort to the hurting, hope to the discouraged and new life to the lost.

Though my only intent was to share it on a single Sunday morning way back in 1999, God had other plans. At the time of this writing, we are in our eighteenth year sharing this letter. My heart now is to share it with you. As far as I am concerned, it is your Heavenly Father who actually wrote the letter. He just used me as His pen.

May these words resonate in the very core of your being so you will know beyond a shadow of a doubt that God loves you and He is the Father you have been looking for all your life.

Father's Love Letter

An intimate message from God to you.

The words you are about to experience are true.
They will change your life if you let them.
For they come from the heart of God.
He loves you.
And He is the Father you have been looking for all your life.
This is His love letter to you.

My child,

You may not know me, but I know everything about you.
Psalm 139:1

I know when you sit down and when you rise up.
Psalm 139:2

I am familiar with all your ways.
Psalm 139:3

Even the very hairs on your head are numbered.
Matthew 10:29-31

For you were made in my image.
Genesis 1:27

In me you live and move and have your being.
Acts 17:28

For you are my offspring.
Acts 17:28

I knew you even before you were conceived.
Jeremiah 1:4-5

I chose you when I planned creation.
Ephesians 1:11-12

You were not a mistake.
For all your days are written in my book.
Psalm 139:15-16

I determined the exact time of your birth
and where you would live.
Acts 17:26

You are fearfully and wonderfully made.
Psalm 139:14

I knit you together in your mother's womb.
Psalm 139:13

And brought you forth on the day you were born.
Psalm 71:6

I have been misrepresented by those who don't know me.
John 8:41-44

I am not distant and angry,
but am the complete expression of love.
1 John 4:16

And it is my desire to lavish my love on you.
1 John 3:1

Simply because you are my child and I am your Father.
1 John 3:1

I offer you more than your earthly father ever could.
Matthew 7:11

For I am the perfect father.
Matthew 5:48

Every good gift that you receive comes from my hand.
James 1:17

For I am your provider and I meet all your needs.
Matthew 6:31-33

My plan for your future has always been filled with hope.
Jeremiah 29:11

Because I love you with an everlasting love.
Jeremiah 31:3

My thoughts towards you are countless
as the sand on the seashore.
Psalms 139:17-18

And I rejoice over you with singing.
Zephaniah 3:17

I will never stop doing good to you.
Jeremiah 32:40

For you are my treasured possession.
Exodus 19:5

I desire to establish you with all my heart and all my soul.
Jeremiah 32:41

And I want to show you great and marvelous things.
Jeremiah 33:3

If you seek me with all your heart, you will find me.
Deuteronomy 4:29

Delight in me and I will give you the desires of your heart.
Psalm 37:4

For it is I who gave you those desires.
Philippians 2:13

I am able to do more for you than you could possibly imagine.
Ephesians 3:20

For I am your greatest encourager.
2 Thessalonians 2:16-17

I am also the Father who comforts you in all your troubles.
2 Corinthians 1:3-4

When you are brokenhearted, I am close to you.
Psalm 34:18

As a shepherd carries a lamb,
I have carried you close to my heart.
Isaiah 40:11

One day I will wipe away every tear from your eyes.
Revelation 21:3-4

And I'll take away all the pain you have suffered on this earth.
Revelation 21:3-4

I am your Father, and I love you even as I love my son, Jesus.
John 17:23

For in Jesus, my love for you is revealed.
John 17:26

He is the exact representation of my being.
Hebrews 1:3

He came to demonstrate that I am for you, not against you.
Romans 8:31

And to tell you that I am not counting your sins.
2 Corinthians 5:18-19

Jesus died so that you and I could be reconciled.
2 Corinthians 5:18-19

His death was the ultimate expression of my love for you.
1 John 4:10

I gave up everything I loved that I might gain your love.
Romans 8:31-32

If you receive the gift of my son Jesus, you receive me.
1 John 2:23

And nothing will ever separate you from my love again.
Romans 8:38-39

Come home and I'll throw the biggest party
heaven has ever seen.
Luke 15:7

I have always been Father, and will always be Father.
Ephesians 3:14-15

My question is...Will you be my child?
John 1:12-13

I am waiting for you.
Luke 15:11-32

Love, Your Dad

Almighty God

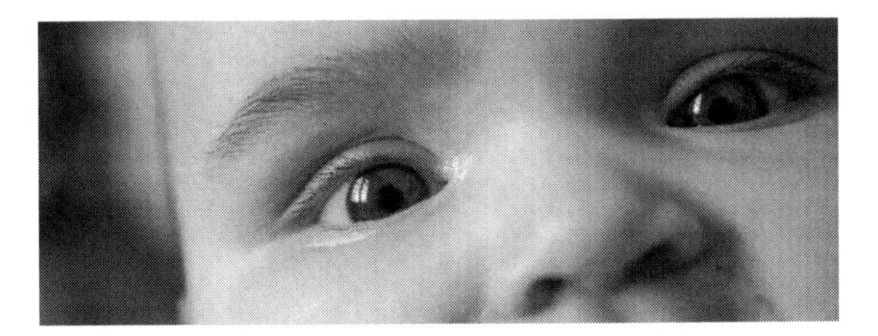

-7-
SHOW US THE FATHER

Our experience sharing the Father's Love Letter has reinforced our belief that the universal cry of the human heart is, "Show us the Father and it will be enough" (John 14:8). I am so glad that Jesus answered that cry in John 14:9 when He replied by saying, "If you have seen me, you have seen the Father."

I believe the more we truly understand the very foundation of the gospel message as a Father's love for us, the more we will see the entire Bible in a new light. As my friend James Jordan says, the Old Testament is simply the story of a Father who lost His kids in a garden (Genesis 3). And the New Testament is the story of the Father's one and only Son, who for love's sake, came to the earth two thousand years ago to get us back (John 3:16).

In 2 Corinthians 5:18-20, we read that God (the Father) was in Christ reconciling the world to Himself, not counting our sins against us. When we see the gospel through the lens of a Father's love, we can truly appreciate the heart behind Jesus' willingness to die on a cross for us. He paid the ultimate price so that you and I could be reconciled to His Father.

As a father myself, I would rather suffer than to see my children suffer. If all fathering comes from God, then the very best expressions of being a dad are but a shadow of the one and only true Father (Ephesians 4:4-6). If I experience pain when I see my children endure hardships, what was the unfathomable price the Father paid in order to secure our redemption?

There is no question that the cross is and will be forever the unshakeable token of the Father's affection. In that moment when Jesus took upon Himself our sin so that we could become the righteousness of God (2 Corinthians 5:21), the Father's grief must have been unimaginable.

Yet the Bible says "it pleased God to bruise Him" (Isaiah 53:10) in order for our everlasting redemption to be secured. Make no mistake about it, the cross represents the greatest price the Godhead could pay in order to make a way for us to come home.

If you have ever questioned God's love for you, you need to look no further than the cross of Christ to see God's sacrificial love in action. 1 John 4:10 says, "This is love: not that we loved God, but that he loved us and sent his Son as an atoning sacrifice for our sins" (NIV).

The Apostle Paul writes these words in Romans 8:31-32:
31 What then shall we say about these things? If God is for us, who can be against us? 32 He who didn't spare his own Son, but delivered him up for us all, how would he not also with him freely give us all things (WEB)?

It was the Father's love initiative to offer up His Son for our redemption. It is the Father who is continually speaking to every heart on the planet about His Son (John 6:44-45). It is the Father who is not willing that even one should perish but that all should come to know Him (2 Peter 3:9). It is the

Father's passion that every person would find their way home to His heart through His beloved Son (John 14:6).

I had a practical experience that helped me gain a tiny understanding of our Father's passion to find those who are lost. It came as I was preparing to go on back-to-back trips to Brazil and Finland. In preparation for the trip, I had to send off my passport to get a Brazilian visa.

I always get a little nervous when I have to entrust my passport to the mail service but I got it back in time for my two trips. Just days before I was about to leave for Brazil, I received a phone call from my friend, Mark, who was going with me. He wanted me to check something on the visa that was in my passport.

When I checked in the normal place where I kept my passport, it wasn't there! I looked everywhere around my house to find it. I remembered that when I got it back in the mail, we were in the midst of doing kitchen renovations and I was afraid I'd placed it in a pile designated for the garbage.

My heart raced as I left my house (after tearing it apart) to go to our office. After tearing my office apart, I was at an intensity level I had never experienced before. The only thing that mattered was finding that passport! It was then I wondered if this might be a teaching moment that Papa wanted me to learn something. So I took a deep breath and told God He had my attention in case He wanted to say something to me.

And of course, that was the case. He said to me these words, "Barry, do you know how you are feeling about your lost passport right now? How you can't think about anything else? How you can't rest until you find it? That is how I feel about everyone who is outside of My house."

At that moment, I was reminded of the stories in Luke 15 of the lost sheep, the lost coin and the lost son. Jesus told these stories to illustrate His Father's unquenchable longing to find that which was lost. My lost passport experience was similar to the lost coin parable Jesus shared in Luke 15:8-10.

8 Or what woman, if she had ten drachma coins, if she lost one drachma coin, wouldn't light a lamp, sweep the house, and seek diligently until she found it? 9 When she has found it, she calls together her friends and neighbors, saying, 'Rejoice with me, for I have found the drachma which I had lost.' 10 Even so, I tell you, there is joy in the presence of the angels of God over one sinner repenting" (WEB).

As soon as I got the message that He wanted to teach me, I asked Papa to show me where my lost passport was. When I returned home, He directed me to a stack of plates. There was my passport securely positioned between two plates.

If you are struggling to relate to God as Father, simply ask Jesus to show you His Father just like Phillip did. For this is the very reason Jesus came to the earth. As you continue to grow in God's amazing love for you, remember that the gospel is gloriously simple. It is a story of a Father who lost His kids in a garden and a Son who came to get us back.

I truly believe that the first words Jesus declared after He rose from the dead will forever express the good news of the Kingdom, not only for His disciples, but for us too.

John 20:17
Jesus said to her, "Don't hold me, for I haven't yet ascended to my Father; but go to my brothers, and tell them, 'I am ascending to my Father and your Father, to my God and your God'" (WEB).

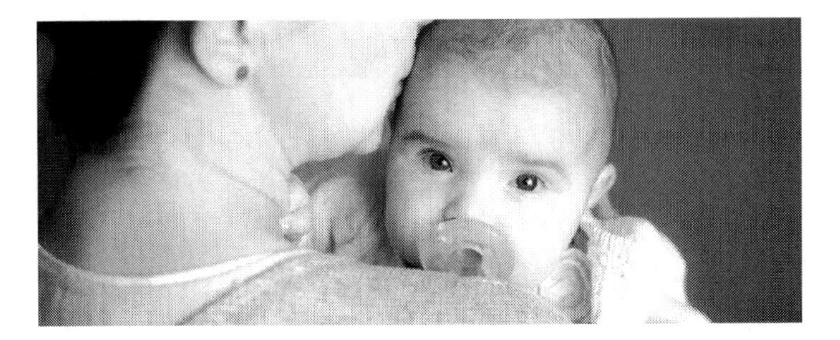

-8-
FAMILY LOVE WITHIN THE GODHEAD

I find it very interesting that all three Persons in the Trinity have relational names. The First Person in the Trinity is called *Father*. You cannot be called *The Fathe*r unless you have a child.

And the same goes for the Second Person in the Trinity. You cannot be called *The Son* unless you have a Father. The Third Person in the Trinity is called both *The Spirit of The Father* (Matthew 10:20) and *The Spirit of The Son* (Galatians 4:4-6).

It was this community of family love that first said in Genesis 1:26 - Let us make man in our image, after our likeness (WEB), and the result was the creation of the human race. It was always the Trinity's intent to include humanity in their ever expanding circle of affection. Adam was called God's son (Luke 3:38) and Eve was the first daughter of the human race.

God's original intent to bring many children to glory (Hebrews 2:10-11) was temporarily delayed in the Garden of Eden when independence was chosen over dependence. But of course, the Godhead had foreseen their disobedience and had already made provision for it by planning the once and for all sacrifice of Christ before the foundation of the world (1 Peter 1:17-21).

So when Jesus came to earth two thousand years ago, we see the fulfillment of the Trinity's original family plan to restore all that was lost in the garden. It is beautiful to see all three Persons of the Trinity in full display at Jesus' baptism.

Matthew 3:16-17
16 Jesus, when he was baptized, went up directly from the water: and behold, the heavens were opened to him. He saw the Spirit of God descending as a dove, and coming on him. 17 Behold, a voice out of the heavens said, "This is my beloved Son, with whom I am well pleased" (WEB).

For the next three years of Jesus' public ministry, the family love of Father, Son and Spirit was fully demonstrated through every loving act that Jesus did. Every person that was drawn to Jesus came at the prompting of the Father (John 6:44-45). Every person that was healed and set free was delivered by the power of the Holy Spirit (Luke 4:14).

Jesus did not even speak one word apart from first hearing His Father speak it (John 12:49) and He only did what He saw His Father doing (John 5:19-20). It was Jesus Christ, the only begotten Son of the Father that brought God to earth in human form.

John 1:14 describes the coming of the Son in this way, "The Word became flesh, and lived among us. We saw his glory, such glory as of the one and only Son of the Father, full of grace and truth" (WEB).

John continues to write in verse 18, "No one has seen God at any time. The one and only Son, who is in the bosom of the Father, he has declared him" (WEB).

How did Jesus declare His Father to the world? By healing every sick person that He met. By feeding the hungry, blessing the little kids, protecting the accused, forgiving the sinners, and raising the dead. And of course, by destroying every judgment, barrier and heavy yoke that religion had created in its attempt to misrepresent the nature of God to the broken and the helpless.

The Apostle Peter describes Jesus' mission in Acts 10:38 by saying, "how God anointed Jesus of Nazareth with the Holy Spirit and power, and how he went around doing good and healing all who were under the power of the devil, because God was with him" (NIV).

Once again, we see the perfect example of God's family love in full display. God the Father anointed God the Son, with the power of God's own Spirit to heal and deliver all those who were under the power of the devil.

In John 8:44, Jesus calls the devil 'the father of lies' and the author of every deception. Satan's intent right from the garden was to question the goodness of God (Genesis 3). Right from the beginning, his plan was to try and entice humanity to live in the illusion of separation and independence from the ultimate source of family love.

In 1 John 3:8, we read that the reason the Son of God came to earth was to destroy the works of the devil. The devil's plan to steal our birthright was annihilated when Jesus rose from the grave.

Our Big Brother's resurrection ushered in a new era for mankind where we could all experience a new birth into the Kingdom of God. As John Calvin said, "The Son of God became the Son of Man, so that the sons of men may become the sons of God."

The intent of the Godhead has always been to restore what was lost in the garden and to bring us back into the indwelling of love that was our original purpose. During the last day of Jesus' life before the cross, He discloses God's divine plan to indwell humanity when He says in John 14:23, 26:

23 "If a man loves me, he will keep my word. My Father will love him, and we will come to him, and make our home with him. 26 But the Counselor, the Holy Spirit, whom the Father will send in my name, he will teach you all things, and will remind you of all that I said to you" (WEB).

We now have complete access to the Father by the Holy Spirit that lives in us (Ephesians 2:18) through our union with Jesus. By virtue of our baptism into Christ (Romans 6:4), we now share in the same relationship that Jesus has with His Father. We don't have to try and cultivate a relationship with God apart from the one that has been freely given to us in the Son.

In Jesus' high priestly prayer in John 17:23, He prays, "I in them, and you in me, that they may be perfected into one; that the world may know that you sent me, and loved them, even as you loved me" (WEB).

The good news is that our union with the Son has given us His union with the Father. Our new birth into God's family (John 1:12-13) has redeemed us and restored us to the original Trinitarian love that was intended to be our birthright in the garden. We are now the dwelling place of the Trinity and recipients of the eternal love that flows between Father, Son and Spirit.

My prayer is that you would know this family love that predates creation (Jeremiah 31:3). I pray you would be awakened to your true destiny as a much loved child of God because of what Jesus did on the cross (Ephesians 1:3-5).

And may you discover in ever-increasing measure who you really are from God's perspective so that you can continue to grow in the family love of God.

The truth that will set you free is that the Trinity is at work in you right now so that the *Abba! Father!* cry might resound in the center of your being!

Romans 8:15-17
15 For you didn't receive the spirit of bondage again to fear, but you received the Spirit of adoption, by whom we cry, "Abba! Father!" 16 The Spirit himself testifies with our spirit that we are children of God; 17 and if children, then heirs; heirs of God, and joint heirs with Christ; if indeed we suffer with him, that we may also be glorified with him (WEB).

-9-
THE NATURE OF A FATHER

The title 'Creator' describes what God does. The name 'Father' describes who He is. Paul writes in Ephesians 4:6 that there is "one God and Father of all, who is over all and through all and in all" (WEB).

I believe that it was always the Father's intent for us to learn to understand what He was like and how we were supposed to relate to Him through our parents. It was always our Abba's heart that we would get a glimpse of His parental affection through this first source of love.

In Isaiah 66:10-13, we read a description of God's mothering heart towards Israel, which is summed up in verse 13, "As a mother comforts her child, so will I comfort you; and you will be comforted over Jerusalem" (NIV).

In Psalm 103:13-14, we read a description of God's fathering heart when King David writes: 13 As a father has compassion on his children, so the Lord has compassion on those who fear him; 14 for he knows how we are formed, he remembers that we are dust (NIV).

Though God is Father, He is the source of all love, both feminine and masculine. He loves us with a maternal, nurturing love that is expressed through the Holy Spirit who is often called the Comforter. And He loves us with a paternal affirming love that helps to establish our identity.

We need both of these expressions of family love in order for us to thrive in life. Without a father's love, we may grow up searching for counterfeit forms of affirmation in our lifelong pursuit of acceptance. Without a mother's love, we may seek out counterfeit forms of comfort to try and fill the hole in our soul.

It is a scientific fact that a deficit of family love can lead to many emotional and physical disorders that plague today's society. If you had loving parents who did their best to show you a healthy expression of family love, that is wonderful because that was God's intent in the first place.

However, if you didn't experience the right kind of family love that God intended because of the brokenness of your own parents, don't despair. Even the best parents' love could only serve as a faint shadow of the love God has for you. If the best parents' love was a drop, your Heavenly Father's love is the ocean.

King David knew a thing or two about disappointment with fathers and father figures. His own dad, Jesse, forgot to invite him to a celebration where one of Jesse's sons was to be anointed king of Israel. And then there was his father-in-law, King Saul, who spent many years trying to kill David as a result of his own insecurities.

Yet in the midst of being let down by father figures, David had a special insight into the heart of God when he wrote in Psalm 27:10, "Though my father and mother forsake me, the Lord will receive me" (NIV).

He also penned the words in Psalm 68:5-6(a): 5 A father to the fatherless, a defender of widows, is God in his holy dwelling. 6 God sets the lonely in families, (NIV).

By the time Jesus arrived on the scene centuries later, the idea of God being a Father was terribly misrepresented and distorted. The religious leaders of the day portrayed God as so holy that they could not even say His name out loud. Yet, when Jesus was speaking to the every day, ordinary folks of that time, He taught them to pray starting with the words, "Our Father who is in heaven'" (Matthew 6:9-13).

Everything Jesus did was the expressed will of His Father (John 6:38-39). He did this so that the tax collectors and sinners could put a face on what God was really like. It was Jesus' passion to make His Father known to a people who had seen God's nature misrepresented by broken earthly fathers and religious leaders alike.

Since 1 John 4:16 tells us "God is love," it only stands to reason that Jesus was love personified on earth. The biblical description of love we find in the Bible comes from 1 Corinthians 13:4-8(a):

4 Love is patient and is kind; love doesn't envy. Love doesn't brag, is not proud, 5 doesn't behave itself inappropriately, doesn't seek its own way, is not provoked, takes no account of evil; 6 doesn't rejoice in unrighteousness, but rejoices with the truth; 7 bears all things, believes all things, hopes all things, endures all things. 8 Love never fails (WEB).

If God is love, I think it is safe to say we could replace the word *love* with the word *God* in this definition of love. And to go one step further, if God is Father, I think we could use the word *Father* in place of love to get a more personal glimpse into His fathering heart too.

Father is patient and is kind; *Father* doesn't envy. *Father* doesn't brag. *Father* is not proud. *Father* doesn't behave inappropriately. *Father* doesn't seek His own way. *Father* is not provoked. *Father* takes no account of evil. *Father* doesn't rejoice in unrighteousness, but rejoices with the truth. *Father* bears all things, believes all things, hopes all things, endures all things. *Father* never fails.

Jesus came to bring us back into relationship with the source of all love, and that was His Dad. There is no question that the New Testament name of God is Father. It is important for us to realize the name *Father* is completely and absolutely relational. The only ones that can call a person 'father' are his children.

If we are trying to understand our value to God based on a broken orphan-hearted world system, the idea of being childlike will hold no value to us.

After all, little children are often overlooked in our society. They have nothing to offer but themselves. They are viewed as the least among us who are weak and helpless. Since they don't earn an income, they can't contribute by paying taxes. They aren't educated or powerful or influential.

They need to be clothed, fed, changed, entertained, provided for, protected and carried around everywhere. If we try to understand their value from a productivity perspective, they are a huge drain on all of our physical, financial and emotional resources.

So if you look at the cold hard facts of what a little child can offer, they will always be found wanting. BUT, if you look at a little child through the eyes of their loving parents, they are the very center of the parents' universe.

A loving parent is not concerned in the least that their little one is completely dependent upon them and they do not consider them a burden. For love's sake, all of their resources are ready, willing and able to nourish, protect, nurture, comfort, encourage and entertain their little ones and provide all they need when they need it. That is the true heart of any loving father or mother.

So as we unpack what it means to live this life as a child of Almighty God, it is important we understand that He sees us through the lens of His family love. We are not a burden to Him and He is not looking for us to 'up our game' and produce to prove our worth.

In God's eyes, we are His much loved little ones who have free access to all of the resources of heaven, simply because He is our Dad. So my prayer is that you would know beyond a shadow of a doubt that your value to your Heavenly Father is beyond measure. He proved His love for you when He emptied the bank to secure your salvation.

He is not just a 'father figure'. He promises to be a real Dad to you. In 2 Corinthians 6:18, Paul writes of a promise that God makes to YOU. "And, I will be a Father to you, and you will be my sons and daughters, says the Lord Almighty" (NIV).

May you continue to see yourself as His beloved child through and through. May you grow in your identity as a son or daughter and know that God does not see you as a slave, but one of His heirs.

The Apostle Paul wrote in Galatians 4:6-7: 6 Because you are his sons, God sent the Spirit of his Son into our hearts, the Spirit who calls out, "Abba, Father." 7 So you are no longer a slave, but God's child; and since you are his child, God has made you also an heir (NIV).

If your earthly parents have misrepresented God's loving heart to you, I pray that God would give you the grace to forgive them for not being the parents you needed. May the comforting love of God's nurturing heart bring healing to every area in your heart that has been damaged by an absence of true love.

I pray you would be so filled with the revelation that Almighty God is your true Father that you would be able to shout the words King David declared in Psalm 27:10, "Though my father and mother forsake me, the Lord will receive me" (NIV).

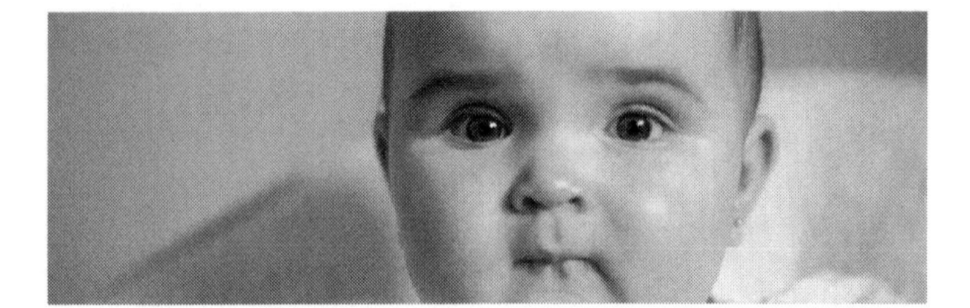

-10-
THE NATURE OF A CHILD

If the Godhead is a family and we have been called to relate to God through family love, the only way we can do that is to posture our hearts as part of the family. If God is Father and Jesus is our Big Brother (Romans 8:29; Hebrews 2:10-11), it only makes sense that our place in the family is as Abba's much loved kids.

While there are many beautiful expressions of our corporate unity (Body of Christ, Bride of Christ, army of God, etc.), our individual identity is and will forever be as sons and daughters. In Ephesians 3:14-15, we read about this amazing family that we have been born into when Paul writes: 14 For this cause, I bow my knees to the Father of our Lord Jesus Christ, 15 from whom every family in heaven and on earth is named, (WEB).

Though we may be entrusted with ministry gifts (apostles, prophets, teachers, evangelists, pastors - Ephesians 4:11-12), God never intended for these gifts to become our identity. These gifts are intended to serve us and the Body on this side of heaven, but they are temporary. The identity that will last forever is the one where all heaven sees us as children of the

Most High (1 John 3:1). It is the heirs of salvation the angels tend to (Hebrews 1:14), not pastors, teachers or prophets.

If you put this in a natural perspective of family life, it becomes quite obvious. I am a father to my kids. First and foremost, I relate to them as my children. Throughout their lives, they may have career changes, but no matter what they 'do' for a living, I will always relate to them relationally as my little ones. Though functionally they work as marketing directors, dental hygienists and sales coordinators, from a dad's vantage point, they are my kiddies!

Could you imagine how absurd it would be if my point of contact with God would be as an itinerant speaker? While that seems absurd, often in church life, we tend to gravitate towards roles and responsibilities rather than relational paradigms. Somehow we think the title of 'apostle' is more prestigious than that of simply being a son or daughter of the living God.

Jesus dealt with this disconnection during His ministry time when He asked His disciples what the crowds were saying about Him. We pick up the conversation in Matthew 16:13-17:

13 When Jesus came to the region of Caesarea Philippi, he asked his disciples, "Who do people say the Son of Man is?" 14 They replied, "Some say John the Baptist; others say Elijah; and still others, Jeremiah or one of the prophets." 15 "But what about you?" he asked. "Who do you say I am?" 16 Simon Peter answered, "You are the Messiah, the Son of the living God." 17 Jesus replied, "Blessed are you, Simon son of Jonah, for this was not revealed to you by flesh and blood, but by my Father in heaven (WEB).

As this story illustrates, people were trying to relate to Jesus based on His function. Because Jesus prophesied, they assumed

He might be a prophet. He asked Peter the same question and Peter answered, "You are the Messiah, the Son of the living God."

My own paraphrase of Jesus' response is, 'BINGO! Peter you got it! You see beyond my function into my core identity as a Son! This revelation was given to you directly from my Father in heaven!' You see, Jesus' entire life was about being a Son, and He was so thrilled that His 'thick' disciples were finally beginning to see that.

If the calling of the Christian life is to be conformed into the image of the Son (Romans 8:29), we also will draw our identity from relationship rather than our function. And that, my friend, brings me to the very point of this book.

People have asked me how I practically live in the love of God. So this is my very best effort to simply share with you what I am learning myself. Jack Winter used to say, "We are three year olds teaching two year olds." I am very comfortable with that description. As far as I am concerned, the more I can 'grow down' and embrace the simplicity of a childlike heart, the more I will 'grow up' in the ways of my Heavenly Papa.

If only a child has the full rights to call God their Abba (Papa, Daddy, Dad, or Father), I want to fully embrace all of the wonders of being a little boy with a really BIG Dad.

I invite you to come alongside of me on this journey to discover how huge and wonderful the Kingdom of God is through the eyes of a much loved, little child.

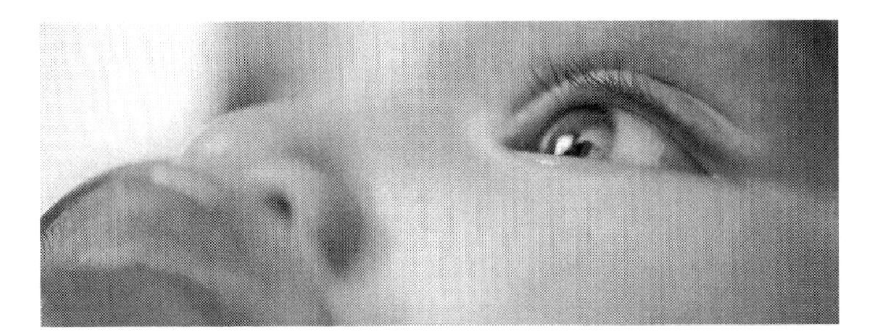

-11-
THE KINGDOM BELONGS TO LITTLE CHILDREN

Jesus spoke about the Kingdom of God more than anything else. We know the proclamation of the Kingdom was meant to be very good news to the hearers (Matthew 24:14). We know the Kingdom is forcefully advancing (Matthew 11:12), it cannot be shaken (Hebrews 12:28-29), it drives out darkness (Luke 11:20) and it is not of this world (John 18:36).

Righteousness, peace and joy are charter members of God's Kingdom (Romans 14:17) and it is the poor of this world that will inherit it (James 2:5). Jesus told us the Kingdom was near (Matthew 10:5-7) and its home address was in the heart of people (Luke 17:20-21).

In this day and age, we hear much talk about God's Kingdom. Conferences that focus on bringing God's Kingdom to earth are usually well attended. So there is no question that as believers, we need to take notice of all things pertaining to seeing God's Kingdom revealed here on earth.

When you think of Kingdom things, what comes to mind? Miracles? Gifts of the Spirit? Profound teachings? Acts of mercy? If you said yes to any of these things, you would be absolutely right. These expressions of heaven on earth are all part of the Kingdom Jesus has conferred on us (Luke 22:29).

But before I go any further, I think it would be helpful for us to remember who the Kingdom belongs to. In order to better understand the qualifications for being great in God's Kingdom (Matthew 18:1-5), we need to go to Luke 18.

This is where parents are lining up to have Jesus hold their little babies and bless them. Meanwhile, Jesus' self-appointed bodyguards (*ahem*, I mean His disciples) were preventing the little babies from coming to Jesus.

I am sure they had the best of intentions, as they didn't want these insignificant little ones to waste their Master's time. I am pretty confident a leader of the Sanhedrin wouldn't have been treated the way the children were, but these were little kids after all.

At this point in time, Jesus' disciples were still seeing through an earthly paradigm of what the Kingdom was all about. As far as they were concerned, these little children were more of a nuisance and a distraction to more important things. So let's read how Jesus handled the situation.

Luke 18:15-17
15 They were also bringing their babies to him, that he might touch them. But when the disciples saw it, they rebuked them. 16 Jesus summoned them, saying, "Allow the little children to come to me, and don't hinder them, for God's Kingdom belongs to such as these. 17 Most certainly, I tell you, whoever doesn't receive God's Kingdom like a little child, he will in no way enter into it" (WEB).

I think this account is pretty self-explanatory. Jesus is crystal clear in what He is saying here. The Kingdom of God belongs to little kids. He wasn't speaking metaphorically here because when He said 'little children', He meant 'little children'.

This must have short circuited the disciple's wiring of what was really important. Think of Jesus' statement, "The Kingdom belongs to children." If it belongs to them, that must mean they have ownership in the Kingdom.

Could you imagine a company's board of directors being filled with two year olds? I kind of think that is what Jesus was saying, and in case the disciples missed it, He made it very personal to them when He said: "Most certainly, I tell you, whoever doesn't receive God's Kingdom like a little child, he will in no way enter into it."

So there you have it. If we want to be people of the Kingdom, if we want to operate in all of the power of the Kingdom, if we want to be considered great in the Kingdom, there is only one way to be able to comprehend its immeasurable vastness, and that is to receive the Kingdom just like a little child would.

Jesus doesn't say you receive the Kingdom like a little child and then you grow up again. He says the only way you can experience all of the practical benefits of Kingdom life is to stay little! There is no question that the Kingdom belongs to little kids and to those who have humbled themselves to become little again.

You may be asking why this is so important to God? After all, this is not how the grown up world works. I am sure Jesus' disciples had the same concerns as many of us do today. It simply doesn't make rational sense to think that babes are the majority shareholders in Papa's estate...but they are!

If we are still trying to understand God's Kingdom through a worldly kingdom perspective, we will never make sense of this. It is only when we return to the place of having the trust and vulnerability of a little child that we will be able to comprehend the mind-bending magnitude of the Kingdom our Papa wants to give us (Luke 12:32).

The Kingdom is simply too big for an adult mind to comprehend. It is only when we choose to change and humble ourselves that we will be able to throw off all of the adult limitations that keep us imprisoned. When we abandon what we think is possible and embrace a childlike perspective, that is the place where nothing will be impossible (Matthew 17:20).

Remember, when Jesus taught His disciples to ask for the Kingdom to come, it was prefaced by the words, "Our Father, who art in heaven…" It is only little kids who know they have a Father in heaven that can ask for His Kingdom to come. It is only little kids who can innocently receive the Kingdom and all its glory that will truly be able to manifest its beauty and power here on earth.

I don't know about you, but I am very glad the Kingdom belongs to little kids!

Matthew 6:9-13
9 Pray like this: 'Our Father in heaven, may your name be kept holy. 10 Let your Kingdom come. Let your will be done, as in heaven, so on earth. 11 Give us today our daily bread. 12 Forgive us our debts, as we also forgive our debtors. 13 Bring us not into temptation, but deliver us from the evil one. For yours is the Kingdom, the power, and the glory forever. Amen (WEB).

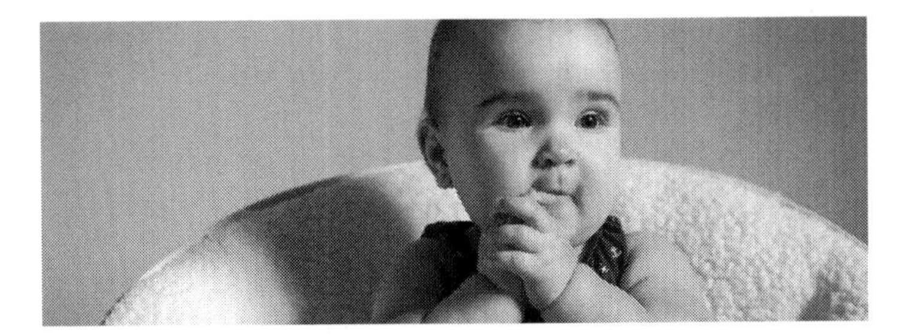

-12-
CHILDLIKE NOT CHILDISH

When I talk about embracing a childlike heart, I want to be clear that I am not talking about childishness. Of course every little child can be childish at times, but the Kingdom attribute that is of great value in the sight of God is a childlike heart.

The reality is childishness is not only reserved for little children. Some of the most childish people I know are not little kids. Childishness in an adult has its root in narcissism and immaturity where they demand everything goes their way. The Kingdom doesn't belong to the childish. It belongs to the childlike.

As I mentioned earlier, we are all called to mature in Christ and grow in our God given destiny. At our new birth, we begin like newborn infants longing for the pure spiritual milk that causes us to grow up in our salvation (1 Peter 2:2) and we mature until we can handle solid food (Hebrews 5:12-13).

But no matter how much we grow up spiritually, from God's perspective, we remain His little ones because the father/child relationship is relative.

Here's an example from my own life. When my children were little, I was in my late twenties. At the time of this writing, our oldest daughter is now in her thirties and is a mother herself. However, when I look at her, I still see my little 8-month-old sweetie who got her photo taken in a beautiful red velvet dress.

You see, no matter how old she gets, I am that much older and my father's heart for her will never change. I fully expect I will still have the same heart for her thirty years from now when she is in her sixties and is a grandmother.

So whether you are two years old or one hundred and two years old, the Ancient of Days who has had no beginning still sees you as His little one!

We can see this very clearly in the way Yahweh relates to the children of Israel in Isaiah 46 where He talks about how He has carried the nation of Israel from the time of their birth to their old age (Isaiah 46:3-4).

I especially like that God mentions that He is still the One who is carrying them in their old age and gray hairs. My prayer is that Abba would give you the wisdom and show you the pathway to return to a childlike awe and wonder in His Kingdom.

Isaiah 46:3-4
3 "Listen to me, you descendants of Jacob, all the remnant of the people of Israel, you whom I have upheld since your birth, and have carried since you were born. 4 Even to your old age and gray hairs I am he, I am he who will sustain you. I have made you and I will carry you; I will sustain you and I will rescue you" (NIV).

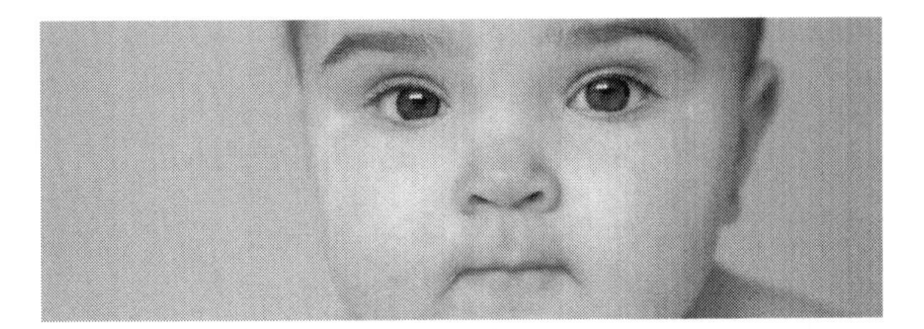

-13- ATTRIBUTES OF A CHILD

Matthew 18:1-5
1 In that hour the disciples came to Jesus, saying, "Who then is greatest in the Kingdom of Heaven?" 2 Jesus called a little child to himself, and set him in the middle of them, 3 and said, "Most certainly I tell you, unless you turn, and become as little children, you will in no way enter into the Kingdom of Heaven. 4 Whoever therefore humbles himself as this little child, the same is the greatest in the Kingdom of Heaven. 5 Whoever receives one such little child in my name receives me, (WEB).

I find it interesting that when the disciples asked Jesus who was the greatest in the Kingdom of heaven, He simply presented a little child and invited them to take a look. Jesus didn't go into a long, complicated sermon about the intricacies of childlikeness; He just pointed to the little one and basically said, here is the best example of true greatness that I can show you!

And Jesus didn't need to go searching for that special child that would be worthy of His sermon illustration because any little kid would do. It is absolutely amazing that there is something woven into the hearts of little children that God finds wonderfully delightful. If He thinks little kids are spectacular, perhaps it would be wise if we observed some of the attributes of little children ourselves so we can learn from them.

Over the following pages, you will read about some of the childlike characteristics that have helped my wife and I walk through this life together. This is by no means an exhaustive list, but it is a good start.

From my own personal experience, I have learned more from my little granddaughter Riley in her first year of life than I could have by reading a thousand books. Being a grandpa to her this past year has been one of the greatest joys of my life. She has taught me so many things in her little life that have reaffirmed my own belief that the Kingdom of God does indeed belong to little children.

Riley was born six weeks after our youngest daughter Candice was diagnosed with Leukemia. We believe her arrival on planet earth was very timely for us as a family as we have had to walk through the most difficult season of our lives.

On the day of her birth, we were at a cancer hospital in the morning with Candice and at a maternity ward in the evening with the whole family. Never before have we experienced such a spike in our emotions in one single day.

But the amazing thing is that God has used our little Riley to bring much love and light to our family in the midst of everything we have experienced. She has brought us great joy and is a daily reminder to our entire family of the very best expressions of Papa's Kingdom here on earth.

On many occasions, I have been completely overwhelmed with a sense of God's presence just looking into her beautiful eyes.

Her innocence, her authenticity and her tender open heart are but a few of the characteristics in her little life that I want to grow down to experience myself.

With the permission and blessing of her amazing parents, Kristin and Nick, I have decided to include some photos of Riley's first year of life.

Special thanks to them for capturing so many beautiful expressions of Riley and for allowing me to use them in this book. I think each one of these photos serve as a real life example of who our Dad considers greatest in His Kingdom. Of course, as a grandpa I am very biased and rightly so!

I hope you will be able to see the value in changing so you can become little again. For the smaller you can be in your heart, the bigger your Heavenly Father can be on your behalf.

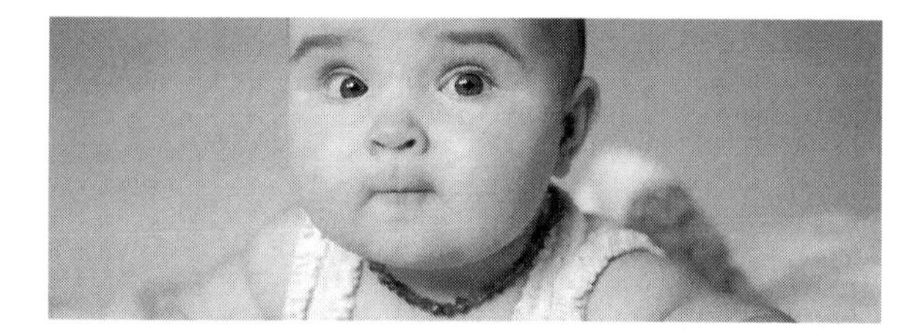

-14-
LITTLE CHILDREN HAVE REALLY BIG HEARTS

There is no question that the heart of a little child is absolutely huge. I am not speaking of their physical heart, but rather the heart which is connected to their mind, will and emotions. I could use the word 'soul' here, but I like the imagery and tenderness that the heart description evokes.

If I could illustrate this in proportion to a baby's body, their intuitive heart would be even bigger than their body. I believe this is the case because we are closest to God's original intent at the time of our birth.

I am not negating that we are all born in sin because of the fall. What I am saying here is that each one of us has a unique design and personality that has been woven into our DNA when God knit us together in our mother's womb (Psalm 139:13).

We are all born with these God designed unique traits that He intended to blossom in a loving environment of parental love. I believe our intuitive hearts are larger than life at this point and are just waiting for a loving world to reinforce and affirm God's design in us (Psalm 139:14).

However, because of the fall and the broken world system we live in, often we see these God-given gifts and personality traits shut down or stolen. The blank slate of our big open heart that was created to be written on by loving parents is often scribbled on with words of judgment, pain and rejection instead.

I believe it has always been God's plan that as we grew up physically, our inner heart would keep pace with our physical bodies. However, instead of flourishing and growing in proportion to our enlarging physical bodies, something inside of us shuts down and our inner heart shrinks.

Before we know it, we become adults trying to live in an orphan world system that has no concept of a Father who is the source of every good thing (James 1:17), so our hearts become very small and closed off.

It is in this process that we lose connection with our heart's desires and all of God's dreams and passions He wove into our DNA. Instead of us reflecting His unique image like He intended (Genesis 1:26-27), we live a life of conformity to other people's expectations and our heart continues to shrink. As a result, the bigger most people become, the smaller their inner hearts become.

I do not believe this was God's plan from the beginning. His intent in the Garden was that Adam and Eve would walk with Him in the cool of the day, naked and unashamed, reflecting God's unique image in all they did.

Before the fall, they had big, open hearts that drank completely from the fountains of God's goodness every moment of every day. But after the fall, their spiritual hearts closed off to all of the delights they enjoyed in the Garden of God. That is when they began to experience the devastation of heart that sins brings.

But the good news of the gospel is that God has given us complete restoration to all that was lost in the garden. When the last Adam came (1 Corinthians 15:45), He paved the way for a new species of sons and daughters (2 Corinthians 5:17) that would share His own divine nature. And that's us!

Over the years, I have found it interesting that many people who have received a deep healing revelation of Father's love seemed to return to the place of a little child in their hearts during their ministry time. I know this hasn't been the case for everybody but it has happened enough for me to take notice of.

I know for me personally, when Jack Winter asked me if I could be a little boy that needed to be loved, I immediately went to a place in my heart where I felt like a broken little five year old. I think the reason this happens to some folks is they are able to get in touch with the child that is already part of them.

If you think of your life like growth rings in a tree, it will be easier to understand. Every ring in the tree represents one year of growth. Some rings are thicker than others because of an abundance of nourishment. Each one of those rings is part of the tree as a whole and the same goes for us.

When a little child turns five, they do not abandon the first four years of their life. They just add one more year to four. Whether we are fifty-five or one hundred and five, our formative years are still a big part of who we are today. When Father pours out His love and we feel like a little kid again, He is touching one of the growth rings in our life that need to be loved.

I can remember a story of a man who was at one of the schools I was teaching at where he went to bed one night and he felt a wave of Father's love come over him. He asked the Lord,

"What was that?" And the Lord answered, "I'm loving the one year old in you right now. Is that okay?" And of course the man said, "yes."

And another wave of love came, and the Lord said, "I'm loving the two year old in you, is that okay?" And for the rest of the night, wave upon wave of God's love touched this man for every year of his life.

Because of the many hurts and pains of childhood, many of us have lost the childlike ability to live with a really big, open heart. But my encouragement to you is that it is still possible by the grace of God to return to a place of living from a childlike heart in the safety of Abba's embrace.

If there is something stirring within you that has a desire to rediscover the little child that is still alive and well within you, ask God for His help. He will gently guide you to a safe and secure place where His love will cause your heart to open up and blossom. The picture that comes to mind is a flower's response to the warmth of the morning sun.

My prayer is that you would ask the Father to lead you back to that place of a little child with a really big, open heart. I pray you would be assured that there is no safer place on earth where you can be little again than in the arms of Almighty God.

Ephesians 1:17-18
17 I keep asking that the God of our Lord Jesus Christ, the glorious Father, may give you the Spirit of wisdom and revelation, so that you may know him better. 18 I pray that the eyes of your heart may be enlightened in order that you may know the hope to which he has called you, the riches of his glorious inheritance in his holy people, (NIV)

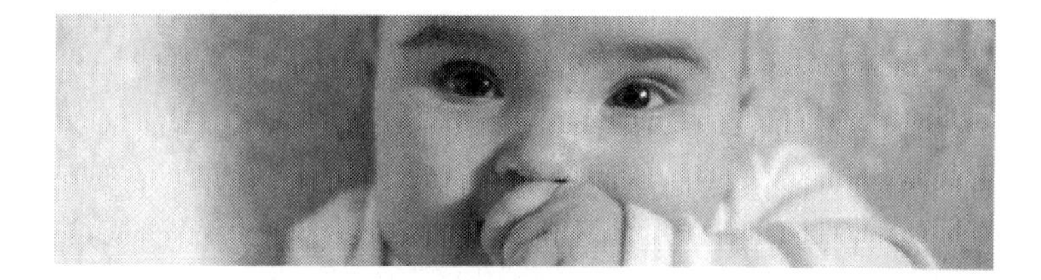

-15-
LITTLE CHILDREN ARE GOOD RECEIVERS

If Christmas or birthdays were every day, little kids would be absolutely over the moon excited when each day came around. The reason they are so excited about gifts is because they are amazing receivers.

Since they cannot do anything for themselves, they have no choice but to stay in a constant state of receiving. I think it is fair to say that their entire life is about receiving from their parents. So when someone gives them a gift, there is not even the hint of awkwardness in the transaction. It is only when we age that we struggle with receiving. After all, in the kingdom of this world, nothing comes for free.

You have to work hard for anything you get. And when someone gives you a gift, it is not only humbling, but in many instances, it also comes with strings attached. So much so, that often it is easier for us to be on the giving end than on the receiving end. But this is where the problem lies.

The Kingdom is all about us learning to live in a posture of receiving from God. John the Baptist said in John 3:27, "A man can receive nothing, unless it has been given him from heaven (WEB). When Jesus sent out His disciples to heal the sick, cast out devils and raise the dead, His charge to them was:

Matthew 10:7-8
7 As you go, preach, saying, 'The Kingdom of Heaven is at hand!' 8 Heal the sick, cleanse the lepers, and cast out demons. Freely you received, so freely give (WEB).

There is no question that we are to be extravagant givers, but the secret to giving is learning to receive first so you have lots to give away. Little kids have no problem with this. Their open hearts are always ready, willing and able to receive at every opportunity.

Often our inability to receive as big people is rooted in pride. If we receive something that is undeserved, it positions us in a place of vulnerability. Often our struggles to receive from God are based in this misguided understanding of how the Kingdom is supposed to work.

If we think we have to work hard for everything we get, the grid through which we receive from God is not based on grace (unmerited favor) but on our own works. While this might sound noble enough (think tree of the knowledge of good and evil), it is absolutely destructive when it comes to things that pertain to the Kingdom.

Remember, God resists the proud but gives grace to the humble (James 4:6). It takes humility to receive something you didn't deserve and that is what Paul wrote in Ephesians 2:8-9:
8 for by grace you have been saved through faith, and that not of yourselves; it is the gift of God, 9 not of works, that no one would boast (WEB).

God has freely given everything that we have to us! James 1:17 says, "Every good gift and every perfect gift is from above, coming down from the Father of lights, with whom can be no variation, nor turning shadow" (WEB). Until we get this simple but pivotal understanding of Kingdom life, we will struggle to receive things we didn't work to get.

Think of it this way. If you went into a store and paid two dollars for a cup of coffee, there would be an expectation that you deserve the coffee because you paid for it. But how would you feel if you went into that same coffee shop and one of the clerks came to you and gave you a free coffee?

At that moment, there could be all kinds of feelings you might have. Surprised, humbled, thankful, uncomfortable, awkward, overwhelmed, etc. Some people might not be able to receive it as a free gift and would insist on paying for it.

A little kid would receive that coffee (or maybe chocolate milk) with great joy and would have absolutely no problem if they were given a donut to go alongside of it. The reason they can so freely receive is because there are not any broken mindsets that have been developed yet from their perspective on how life works. They are simply great receivers.

If our ability to receive is based solely on what we think we have earned or deserved, we will severely limit what we can receive from God. Often people struggle to receive God's love for them because they don't think they deserve it. But here's the thing. I can give you a million dollars but that gift doesn't become yours until you receive it.

No matter how much I tell you it now belongs to you, unless you open up your hands and receive what I give, you won't enjoy the benefits of being a millionaire. It's like that with God's plan of salvation.

When Jesus died on a cross, He took upon Himself the sins of the entire world and thereby made a way for everyone to be saved. So in a nutshell, Jesus has already paid the price for every person to live a completely forgiven and free life.

The price has already been paid. The gift has already been given. The only thing that is left is for us to individually receive by faith the free gift of God expressed through the finished work of His Son. But the gift still has to be received in order to be enjoyed.

In John 1:11-13, John writes about this:
11 He came to his own, and those who were his own didn't receive him. 12 But as many as received him, to them he gave the right to become God's children, to those who believe in his name: 13 who were born not of blood, nor of the will of the flesh, nor of the will of man, but of God (WEB).

The tragedy of those who reject Christ is that the free gift of everlasting life and reconciliation to the Father that has already been paid for remains a gift unopened.

I am thankful our Father continues to be patient with us, not wanting anyone to perish (2 Peter 3:9). I believe evangelism is simply telling people about the free gift Papa has already given them that is found in His Son.

Often, the foundation of why we struggle to receive is based on how we were raised as a child. If we were taught that nothing comes for free, we will grow up feeling the need to earn or deserve what we get. If we have had parents that made us feel ashamed for asking for things, it is easy for us to make the misguided assumption that God must be the same way.

I can remember in the early days of our ministry, God had encouraged me to ask for His blessing on my life. While I found it easy to pray for God to bless other people, all of a sudden, I felt a strange awkwardness about asking Papa to bless me personally. But that is what He wanted me to do so I went for it. With a childlike faith and simplicity, I asked Papa to bless me, my family and the works of my hands.

At that time, FathersLoveLetter.com was receiving three thousand visits a day on a regular basis, so I asked God to increase it to ten thousand visits a day. Within one week, without any changes in the way I did anything, we were receiving ten thousand visits a day. Within another week, our web traffic increased again to thirty thousand visits a day and then over a million visits per month!

It was at this moment that the reaches of the love letter really became a global Internet phenomenon. All because a little boy asked His Dad to bless Him.

My prayer today is that you would position your heart like a little child in order to receive every good and perfect gift that comes down from the Father of Lights. May God give you the grace to lay down your adult mindset that only serves to limit you.

May you return to the wonderful place of being just a little boy or girl and get ready to receive all that Papa wants to give you.

Luke 12:32
Don't be afraid, little flock, for it is your Father's good pleasure to give you the Kingdom (WEB).

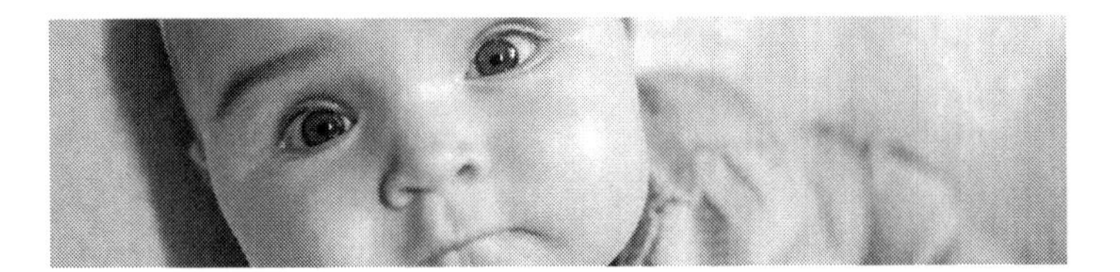

-16-
LITTLE CHILDREN ARE WEAK

There is no question that little children are weak. The smaller they are, the weaker they are. I can remember when I held our granddaughter at the hospital. I was so struck by how vulnerable she was as a newborn. When holding her, I had to be careful if I shifted my position, as her little neck muscles couldn't even hold her head up.

Adults don't like to be weak. Even when we are, we try to hide our weakness from those around us because we often see weakness as vulnerability and inferiority. In a world system that always celebrates the victor, weakness is often looked down upon because we associate it with failure.

I experienced a reasonable amount of success growing up. I was a popular student with good grades. I did reasonably well at the sports I participated in and held my own in the business world. I had a beautiful wife so I thought the world was my oyster.

Then when I was twenty-five years old, I started a part time tourist publishing company that I really thought was a God idea. I even made God my business partner and went ahead and ordered twenty thousand books, which I expected to sell in no time.

While I had success in getting the books placed in almost every tourist shop in Niagara Falls, they didn't sell. Weeks turned into months and all of a sudden, I panicked. Since we were storing our entire remaining inventory of sixteen thousand books in our master bedroom, the whole house smelled like a print shop.

In an effort to twist God's arm into generating more sales, I wrote Bible verses on every box of books and increased my giving, praying and Bible reading. But the harder I worked, the worse things became.

I can remember coming home every night after work to spend time with just God and me in our master bedroom. Surrounded by sixteen thousand unsold books, all I could do was weep before Him. I became so broken and disillusioned that, for a season, I stopped tithing, reading my Bible and even going to church.

While all this was happening, I was also forced to go on eighty-five percent commission at my day job in the newspaper business. With a failing business and a reduced income, it looked like I was not going to be able to have enough money to provide for our family.

It was at this very low point that I truly gave up on my misguided expectations of how God was supposed to bless me. Up until that time, I thought if I looked after His business (church work), He was obligated to look after mine. Yet things weren't working out like I had planned. But then something happened.

When I stopped doing all of the good works I thought would pressure God into blessing me, I braced myself for some harsh discipline from the Lord. But to my surprise, that is when the windows of heaven's blessings poured out on us. My commissioned sales income dramatically increased and God rescued us from our failing business through a financial miracle and the love and kindness of our family. At this point, I became confused.

When I was doing all the 'right things' in hopes that God would bless me, things got worse. But when I was at my lowest point, completely weak and discouraged, I was rescued. One day in prayer, I told the Lord that I didn't deserve all of His blessings and He wholeheartedly agreed. Then I heard Him say, "You've just experienced My grace."

From that moment on, I began to walk with an emotional limp (think of the story in Genesis where Jacob gets his hip socket dislocated by an angel). You see, up until that time, I had a twisted theology of who God was that was based on me playing my part and thus kind of deserving His blessings.

But after this encounter with the love of God, I saw things differently. His love didn't come to me when I was at my strongest. His love came to me at my weakest. Though that encounter with God was nearly thirty years ago, it continues to remind me that it is when I am weak that I am strong.

The Apostle Paul had a similar revelation in 2 Corinthians 12:7-10 when he asked God to take away the thorn in his flesh that was continually buffeting him. After his third request, Jesus Himself appeared to Paul in verse 9 and said, "My grace is sufficient for you, for my power is made perfect in weakness" (WEB).

It was only then that Paul received a revelation of weakness that redefined his idea of strength. He responded in the last half of the verse by saying, "Most gladly therefore I will rather glory in my weaknesses, that the power of Christ may rest on me" (2 Corinthians 12:9). Paul sums up this revelation in verse 10 by saying, "For when I am weak, then am I strong" (WEB).

The reality is that God has always used weak people. Moses stuttered. Gideon hid in a wine vat. King David had a trunk full of imperfections yet he was called a man after God's own heart. It was David who wrote that the sacrifices of God are a broken spirit and a contrite heart (Psalm 51:16-17).

In my own experience, I have discovered that when I try to be strong in my own self-effort, my own strength just gets in the way. However, when I simply embrace the weakness of a little child, I am no longer relying on my own strength. It is in this place of complete surrender that I have the power of the entire universe at my disposal.

Little kids don't struggle with this concept. Without having the ability to even understand the principle of weakness, they simply live in a continual state of helplessness. Yet in this place where a little baby cannot even hold up its own head, this little one has unrestricted access to the strength of their parents. And if our parents are but a shadow of the heart of our Heavenly Father, how much more will He show Himself strong on our behalf?

That is why Paul writes in Ephesians 6:10 that we are to 'be strong in the Lord and in His mighty power.' It is His strength that becomes our strength when we are courageous enough to lay down every counterfeit expression of strength we can muster up.

The good news of the gospel is that God has chosen the weak to confound the strong (1 Corinthians 1:26-29). If you have ever felt poor, weak or foolish, you qualify for being great in Papa's Kingdom.

My prayer is that you would see the glorious freedom that is available when you stop trying to be strong so God can demonstrate just how big He is on your behalf.

Isaiah 40:29
He gives power to the weak. He increases the strength of him who has no might (WEB).

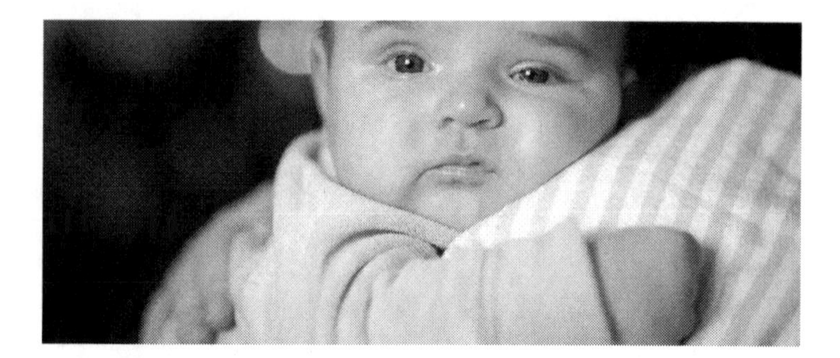

-17-
LITTLE CHILDREN ARE HAPPY TO BE CARRIED

Our granddaughter loves to be carried. Though she is at an age where she gets around on her own, she still loves to be held. Every time we are together, she inevitably wants me to pick her up and there begins our adventure.

Since she is not able to express in words what she wants me to do, she simply points in a direction and grunts. Then off I go in the direction she is pointing. I consider my big strong arms to be her personal chariot that is ready, willing and able to take her wherever she wants to go in our house.

When is the last time you were carried by someone? Chances are it hasn't been a recent memory. As adults, we are the ones usually doing the carrying. We carry little ones, we carry the groceries and sometimes, we carry the weight of the world on our shoulders. Yet, it is Almighty God that tells us He has carried us since our birth.

Earlier in the book, I mentioned Isaiah 46:3-4 where Yahweh is addressing the nation of Israel, and I think it bears repeating:

3 "Listen to me, you descendants of Jacob, all the remnant of the people of Israel, you whom I have upheld since your birth, and have carried since you were born. 4 Even to your old age and gray hairs I am he, I am he who will sustain you. I have made you and I will carry you; I will sustain you and I will rescue you" (NIV).

Do you get that? God says to an entire nation that He has been carrying them all of their lives whether they knew it or not! Even to their gray hair and old age, God has the tender heart of a father that loves to carry His kids around.

The thing is, did the nation of Israel really enjoy the benefits of being carried or were they oblivious to God's nearness to them? I kind of think they were so busy running their own lives that they had lost the awareness of just how close God was and how He was carrying them the whole time.

If the New Covenant is a better covenant than the old one, how much more involved is God in our everyday lives now? How much more would He now want us to know He is a loving Father who is closer than we could imagine?

There was a time in my own life when I experienced a tangible expression of God carrying me. It happened in the early days of our ministry when I was feeling completely overwhelmed by the pressures of having an international influence. My mind was constantly being bombarded by anxious thoughts as I tried to come to grips with seeing the love letter delivered around the world.

I can remember a specific day when I was attending a 'Father Loves You' conference in Toronto. On this particular day, I was feeling especially exhausted. I had just read Hebrews 12:1, "Therefore, since we are surrounded by such a great cloud of witnesses, let us throw off everything that hinders and the sin that so easily entangles. And let us run with perseverance the race marked out for us" (NIV).

I asked Father to help me run my race that day. I told Him I had no more strength and I needed His help to keep running. In one of the afternoon sessions, a friend of mine was speaking and he told a story about a young man named Derek Redmond[1]. He was a British athlete who was running in the semi-final race of the 1992 Olympics in Barcelona.

Early in the race, he pulled a hamstring and yet he still tried to finish the race, limping and grimacing in pain as he rounded the track. All of a sudden, a man ran onto the racetrack and helped him finish the race. It was his father. Arm in arm, both father and son finished the race together.

After my friend finished telling this story, he said sometimes we all get too tired or hurt to finish our own race, and just like in this story, our Heavenly Father runs onto our racetrack to carry us to the finish line. It was like something extremely profound happened right in the very core of my being, and I wept.

At that moment, I had an overwhelming encounter with the love of God that centered me back to what was really important in life. It wasn't my ministry that was important to God; it was me! And as the father in the story was helping his son to the finish line, my Heavenly Dad was carrying me on a day when I had nothing left to give.

Later that evening, another speaker finished his message by telling the story of another father/son race team where the father, Dick Hoyt, pulled, pushed and carried his disabled adult son, Rick Hoyt, to the finish line of the grueling Ironman Triathlon race in Hawaii[2]. He ended his message by playing a video of father and son competing in the race. The dad in his sixties pulled his son on a life raft during the 2.4 mile swim.

Next, he carried his son Rick to a specially outfitted seat for the 112-mile bike ride and then pushed him in a wheelchair for the final 26.2 mile run.

If I didn't get the message earlier in the day when I heard the first story, I did now after watching this living example of a father's love for his son. I completely lost it right then and there, and once again yielded to the wondrous reality that my Dad was carrying me.

That day was a marker for me that I have had to revisit many times since. Oftentimes, I tend to forget I am being carried. It is at these times that I start carrying the weight of the world on my shoulders again.

There was another time when I tore my calf muscle during a squash game and was unable to physically walk. The next day, I was supposed to be interviewed on a national Christian television program and I didn't know how I would be able to get there in my condition. That is when I heard God say to me, "Don't worry son, I'll carry you." Once again, I had a centering moment in the love of my Papa and I wept.

The reality is your Heavenly Father is carrying you whether you know it or not. Simply put, that is what loving dads do for their kids. You don't have to carry the weight of the world on your own shoulders. Just settle back into your Father's big, strong arms and let Him carry you.

Deuteronomy 33:27a
The eternal God is your refuge, and his everlasting arms are under you (NLT).

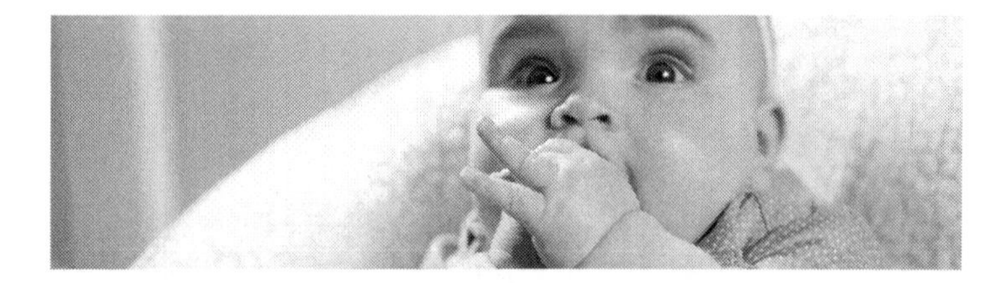

-18-
LITTE CHILDREN ARE CREATIVE GENIUSES

In the 1960s, the National Aeronautics and Space Administration (NASA) asked Dr. George Land to create a test that would help NASA assess the creativity of its engineers[3]. From what I understand, the criteria was to develop a test that would measure a person's ability to look at a problem and come up with new innovative ideas that were *outside of the box*.

The test ended up being highly predictive, so Dr. Land decided to apply the same NASA test to 1600 five year olds to measure their creativity. I watched a Ted Talk of Dr. Land explaining this creativity test, where he shared that to his surprise, 98% of these five year olds were already in the creative genius category[4].

He continued the study of the same group of kids and by the time they were fifteen years old, the genius category dropped to 12%. When you consider that only 2% of the adults tested in this study scored in the genius category, it seems like the obvious conclusion is that our ability to think *outside of the box* actually decreases with age.

When I read about this study, it only deepened my own belief that our ability to dream impossible dreams is something that they we were all born with. If that is the case, then creativity is not something we have to learn, but it is something that 98% of us un-learn.

Thinking extraordinary thoughts is not something that most little kids have to work at. It is as intuitive to them as breathing. However, because of the broken world system that surrounds us, this God given ability is often eroded rather than nurtured.

Picture your own life for a moment. Was there a time in your life when some well meaning parent or school teacher shut down the creative genius inside of you? Maybe somebody told you to stop dreaming? Maybe someone pointed you in a direction away from the things that made you come alive because it just wasn't practical?

I truly believe it is only when we return to the heart of a little child that we will truly be able to believe what our Papa says is true. If we are still thinking like an adult, we will more than likely nullify the impossible with many adult reasons why it isn't possible.

But when we simply believe with childlike faith that nothing is impossible, that's when we once again align ourselves with the realities of the Kingdom of God where mountains are moved on a regular basis.

Einstein said, "Imagination is more important than knowledge."[5] I truly believe what we need as believers today is more imagination and less information. And the only way we can even hope to comprehend the vastness of what God has in store for us is to return to that little boy or girl that has a really big Dad.

In Matthew 11:25-26, Jesus prays this prayer to His Dad:

25 At that time, Jesus answered, "I thank you, Father, Lord of heaven and earth, that you hid these things from the wise and understanding, and revealed them to infants. 26 Yes, Father, for so it was well-pleasing in your sight" (WEB).

If you ever wondered who the mysteries of the Kingdom were revealed to, look no further. Is it the wise and the learned? No way! The Kingdom our Father delights to reveal is so big, so vast, so beyond human understanding that only an '*untaught, unskilled, babe*' (Strong's Greek word definition for infants: *nay'-pee-os*) could actually get it.

And Jesus says it is His Father's absolute delight to reveal His Kingdom to little ones. So my prayer today is that you would take the path less travelled and turn and become a little child again. This is the place where the impossible realm is alive and well.

This is where little kids live every day and are not even aware of the greatness they carry. This is where their rocket ships and far away lands exist. This is where they dream of damsels in distress, knights in shining armor, and other things much too big for the adult mind to grasp.

If our lives are indeed like growth rings in a tree, then there is a five year old inside of you that is just waiting to be released again to the world. He or she may have been banished by adult reasoning to a seldom accessed part of the heart, but all we have to do is open the door to that part of our being and let him or her out.

My prayer is that God will give you wisdom on how to do that. May the Holy Spirit teach you how you can change and become like a little child so He can restore your ability to think outside of the box again.

After all, we live in a Kingdom of magical wonder all around us. Jesus walked on water, passed through walls, healed the sick, raised the dead and even flew during His ascension to heaven. And He told us that we would do greater things than He did because He was going to our Father (John 14:12).

In the realm of God's Kingdom, angels are all around us (Hebrews 1:14) and all of heaven is cheering us on to run our unique race (Hebrews 12:1).

If we don't return to the place of being small again in our hearts, we will find it difficult to believe all this is true. So get ready to receive the Kingdom just like a little child would and open your heart to dream again!

1 Corinthians 2:9-10
9 But as it is written, "Things which an eye didn't see, and an ear didn't hear, which didn't enter into the heart of man, these God has prepared for those who love him." 10 But to us, God revealed them through the Spirit. For the Spirit searches all things, yes, the deep things of God (WEB).

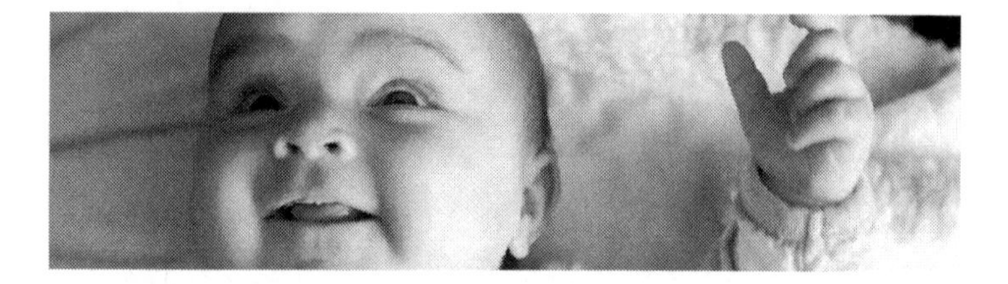

-19-
LITTLE CHILDREN KNOW HOW TO TRUST

Little children are born with trusting hearts. They rely on their parents or care givers for everything they receive. In fact, they have no choice but to trust with all of their little hearts.

It was always God's intent that we would learn to trust Him through the nurturing love we were supposed to receive from our parents. King David speaks of the foundational building block of trust in Psalm 22:9-10:

9 Yet you brought me safely from my mother's womb and led me to trust you at my mother's breast. 10 I was thrust into your arms at my birth. You have been my God from the moment I was born (NLT).

If we had learned to trust like we were supposed to when we were babies, trusting God would be much easier. Unfortunately, the ones God intended to love, protect and cover us were not able to because of the brokenness in their own lives.

Yet, we still opened up our hearts to them because as little ones, we didn't know what else to do but trust them. The result was that our tender, open, trusting hearts began to get hurt at an early age and for good reason, mistrust crept in. Instead of trusting more, we trusted less and less. Instead of having big, open hearts that believed everything and everybody, we became cynical, suspicious and closed hearted.

This was not what our Heavenly Father had in mind for us. In the Garden of Eden, we would all have had undefiled, trusting hearts. There would not have even been one thought of trying to separate good from evil because everything would have been good.

The word 'redemption' means to 'regain possession of something'. When Jesus died on a cross two thousand years ago, He made a way for all of us to be fully restored to what was lost in the Garden. I believe one of the things Jesus came to restore was our ability to trust.

Eight years ago, Ann and I invited some of our dear friends to our house to prophetically speak into our lives. They asked us a bunch of questions about our lives and our ministry. One of the things I was struggling with that I shared was my inability to be at peace when it came to the future.

Since we lived by faith, every month was an adventure in the way God provided for us. Even though He was always faithful, I continually wondered if our ability to live this way would end at any moment.

No matter how much I prayed about this restless, peaceless feeling, I constantly lived with the sense that it all could be taken away at any time. Our friends prayed into this uneasy mindset that I couldn't shake and one of them had a picture.

They saw me as a two-year-old little boy whom God had given a great capacity to trust. However, because of the nature of the home I was raised in, I struggled to entrust myself to the care of my parents. I grew up in a home where the atmosphere was continually changing because of my dad's struggle with alcoholism. This made it difficult for me to find a safe place where I could give my trust to someone. The result was that I became hyper vigilant.

Since I had no place where my trust could be placed, I ended up feeling the need to trust in my own abilities to protect myself from getting hurt. This resulted in a lifetime of self-protection and a never-ending restlessness that was a casualty of not being able to learn how to trust.

Before my friends prayed for me, I told them about a conference I attended years earlier in Holland. The speaker prayed for people after one of his sessions, so I lined up to receive ministry. When he got to me, he touched my stomach and immediately my stomach muscles contracted in a way I had never experienced before.

I was literally bent over with the top of my head on the carpet, which was a very undignified position to be in! I'd never had anything like that happen to me before, but I went with it because in fact, I really had no choice.

A while later, the ministry time was over and people were leaving, so I thought I should get up and join my friends. The only problem was, when I tried to remove the top of my head from the carpet, I couldn't!

By that time, flashes from cameras were going off as people were quite enjoying my unorthodox ministry time posture. It was then that I asked the Lord to let me know what He was doing, and He answered by saying, "Barry, you have a very active thought life, so I am flushing all of your thoughts into the carpet just like you would flush a toilet."

When I was eventually able to unstick my head from the floor, I literally couldn't string two thoughts together! I have to say, this was one of the most wonderful experiences I've ever had. As somebody who could never shut his mind off before that moment, this was a welcome calm in the midst of a never-ending whirlwind of thoughts.

The next day, my inability to process thought continued even though I had to travel with a good friend from Holland to England. I'm so glad my friend Mark was with me that day, as I was not able to process our travel plans without him.

How would we get from the conference center to the train station? I did not know! How would we get to the airport and on to England? I did not know! My friend had to buy my tickets, lead me by the hand and make every decision for me.

Unfortunately, my active thought life did eventually return, but that experience of having all my anxious thoughts flushed was a living reminder of a passage of Scripture that has become very meaningful ever since.

Proverbs 3:5-6
5 Trust in Yahweh with all your heart, and don't lean on your own understanding. 6 In all your ways acknowledge him, and he will make your paths straight (WEB).

I believe that our ability to trust God with all of our heart is directly connected with our ability to not lean on our own understanding. Oftentimes, if we haven't discovered a safe place to establish trust as a little child, we have no choice but to trust in our own understanding to fix every problem.

So the more we learn to trust God, the less we will need to trust in our own human intellect to navigate all of the pitfalls that life will throw at us. Isaiah 26:3 says, "You will keep in perfect peace all who trust in you, all whose thoughts are fixed on you" (NLT).

As my friends prayed into this really big issue of broken trust for me, they had a picture of my Heavenly Father leading me by the hand around train stations and airports just like my friend did.

They encouraged me that my Papa had great adventures for us to go on together and that He wanted me to place my childlike trust in Him so I could enjoy the ride.

It was right then that they ministered to me and asked God to restore basic, childlike trust to me. I can honestly say that this time of personal ministry was very profound but it did not come with an immediate fix to all my trust issues. It was a good start, but I am still a work in progress.

This journey of learning to trust God has been a continuum that I don't think will ever end this side of heaven. I am learning that the words trust, faith and believe are interwoven with each other. I can't have faith in God if I don't trust Him. I can't believe His Word to be true if I don't trust He is good.

If you look at the Greek word for trust (*pist-yoo'-o*), you will see it has similar roots to the word faith (*pis'-tis*). In John 14:1, Jesus comforts His disciples, "Don't let your hearts be troubled. Trust in God, and trust also in me" (NLT). It is this same Greek word (*pist-yoo'-o*) that is used in John 6:29 when Jesus says, "This is the work of God, that you believe in him whom he sent" (WEB).

The whole point of the Christian life is to learn to trust God. Little children are born with this gift and it is only the ravages of sin that pummel our little hearts over and over again until we learn to exchange trust for mistrust.

The good news is our God and Father wants to restore childlike trust to you. He is the One who hard-wired your genetic code so that your default settings would be to trust and He is the One who can restore those settings.

I believe the way to restoration involves returning to the place where you lost trust in the first place. And that is when you were little. Instead of having to trust in fickle, broken parents, this time you get to place your trust in the biggest, most loving Dad in the universe.

My prayer is that God would show you how trustworthy He is. 2 Timothy 2:13 says, "if we are faithless, he will remain faithful, for he cannot disown himself" (NIV). So my friend, even when you struggle to believe in Him, He continues to believe in you.

There is a story in Mark 9:17-29 where a father asked Jesus to heal his son, and Jesus responds with the question, "Do you believe?" and the man answered, "Lord, I believe, help my unbelief!"

It would be like us saying Lord, I trust you, but please help me in the areas where I still don't trust. This honest declaration from this father who wanted his son healed was enough for Jesus, and this honest declaration is enough for us too.

My prayer is that you would see how valuable your ability to trust God is to Him. When we get to heaven, we will have no need for a trust that is rooted in faith because we will see God face to face. But on this side of heaven, when we are facing all sorts of hardships and obstacles that will attempt to tell us that God isn't trustworthy, we have the privilege of learning to trust Him. I believe it is at these times our childlike trust completely blesses our Dad's heart.

Over the years, I have had many opportunities to learn to trust God. I have had to trust God with my finances, my ministry and my future.

It seems as I learn to trust Him in one area, I see other areas in my life that are still rooted in mistrust and unbelief. I am so thankful that my Papa keeps on loving me through each and every hurdle I face.

These past eighteen months have exposed an area in my heart where I have had to trust God like never before. In September 2014, our youngest daughter, Candice, was diagnosed with Acute Lymphocytic Leukemia (ALL).

As a dad, I was devastated and very worried for my daughter as any father would be. There were many sleepless nights in the early days of her diagnosis where I battled fear and anxiety. I could not stop the recurring thoughts of fear and worry that kept me void of peace. One morning, Papa spoke very clearly to me, "Barry, can you trust Me with Candice?"

In this moment, I realized God was a Father to my daughter more than I could ever be, so He was worthy of my trust. At that point, I was able to entrust my daughter into the loving care of my Abba and peace was immediately restored to me.

Now to be clear, that does not mean there haven't been some bumps in the road, because there have been lots. But with each challenge in life comes an invitation to trust.

My prayer is that we would all learn to trust God intuitively again, just like little kids. May we find all of the comfort that we need in His big, strong arms knowing that He has promised to care for us like no father on earth could ever do.

1 John 4:16
We know how much God loves us, and we have put our trust in his love. God is love, and all who live in love live in God, and God lives in them (NLT).

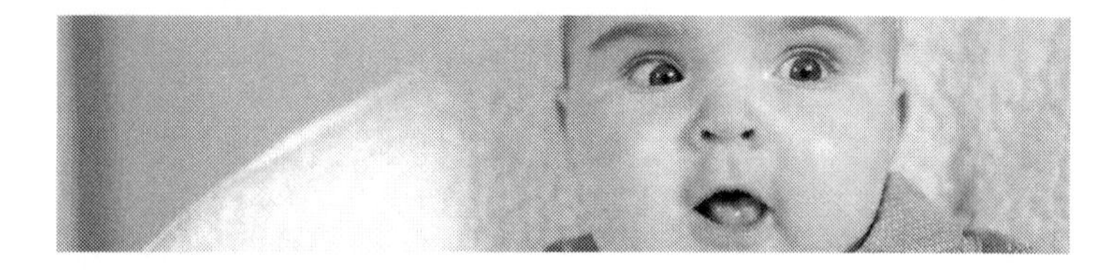

-20-
LITTLE CHILDREN DO WHAT THEY ARE TOLD

Little kids don't question authority, at least when they are very small. They realize they don't know very much, so they are continually learning what to do and what not to do. Our granddaughter is at a stage right now where she is crawling all over the place and exploring every new experience that she can.

Seeing, smelling, touching and often trying to taste things are the ways she is learning about the world around her. All of this is happening under the watchful eye of her loving family, so it is a safe place for her to learn. I find it hilarious how she will now approach something new and look back at us to see how we will respond.

If it is something safe for her to explore, we encourage her to experience it in all its glory. If it is something unsafe, we will tell her *no*. I'm not saying our little Riley is the perfect grandchild and does everything she is told, but she is definitely well on her way. I'm amazed at the humility I see in her as she pulls her hand back after hearing the words, "No, Riley. Don't touch."

Obedience is a very important part of the child/parent relationship. It begins with the fundamental understanding that the parent knows best and has the child's best interests at heart. A classic example of this is when a parent tells a little child not to touch a hot stove because of the consequences of being burned.

Obedience not viewed through the grid of a loving family relationship will end up being a harsh, legalistic set of rules we are required to follow. The reality of life is that I can keep all the rules and still not love but I can't love completely without keeping the very spirit of the law's intent. That is why love is the fulfillment of the law as Paul wrote in Romans 13:10.

If we know that our Heavenly Father loves us with all His heart, we can trust His direction without ever having to question His motives. Jesus, as the perfect Son, modelled this in everything He did. In John 6:38, we clearly see Jesus' heart of obedience. "For I have come down from heaven, not to do my own will, but the will of him who sent me" (WEB).

When love is our greatest aim (1 Corinthians 14:10), obedience to God is our absolute delight (Psalm 40:8). We can see love and obedience woven together in John 15:9-10: 9 Even as the Father has loved me, I also have loved you. Remain in my love. 10 If you keep my commandments, you will remain in my love; even as I have kept my Father's commandments, and remain in his love (WEB).

I think one of the greatest problems in the Christian life is our resistance to obedience. In today's culture, the word 'obedience' is almost considered inappropriate as it is painted with all things related to religion gone bad. And to be honest, we have seen lots of religious abuse to fuel that school of thought.

However, in the context of love, obedience is simply one of the most beautiful expressions we can manifest. Jesus saw obedience to His Dad as His very sustenance when He said in John 4:34, "My food is to do the will of him who sent me, and to accomplish his work" (WEB). His mission was to always do the things that pleased His Father (John 8:29).

My prayer is that we would see obedience through the lens of family love. May we never fall in the trap that Adam and Eve fell into when they bought into the lie of the serpent that questioned God's goodness (Genesis 3:1-5).

God always has your best interests at heart. He loves you with an everlasting love (Jeremiah 31:3) and He has a bright future in store for you (Jeremiah 29:11).

May His love vanquish any lies about His goodness and may His grace give you the ability to return to the place of a little child that simply does what they are told. May your obedience be a testimony that you love your Father and you do what He says just like your Big Brother does.

John 14:30-31
30 "I don't have much more time to talk to you, because the ruler of this world approaches. He has no power over me, 31 but I will do what the Father requires of me, so that the world will know that I love the Father. Come, let's be going (NLT).

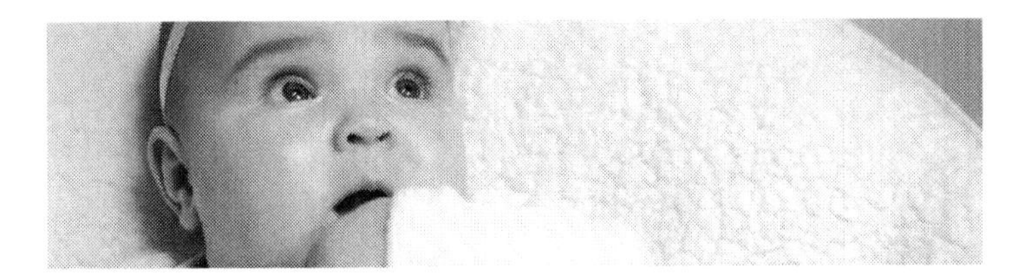

-21-
LITTLE CHILDREN ARE HAPPY TO BE LED

Little children are happy to be led by their parents. They are not carrying around an adult sized independence that causes them to resist and rebel. They simply follow because they know in their little hearts they are not able to lead themselves.

I find it interesting that one of the signs of sonship in the Bible focuses on our ability to be led. Romans 8:14 says, "For as many as are led by the Spirit of God, these are children of God" (WEB).

Think about the ramifications of this statement. In order for us to be led, we need to be in a posture of waiting to be led. All self-generated initiative is inactive when we are waiting to be led. The Bible has much to say about the rewards for those who wait.

Psalm 37:34
Wait for Yahweh, and keep his way, and he will exalt you to inherit the land. When the wicked are cut off, you shall see it (WEB).

Isaiah 64:4
For from of old men have not heard, nor perceived by the ear,

nor has the eye seen a God besides you, who works for him who waits for him (WEB).

When we position our hearts to be in a place where we acknowledge that God is our source and only He can rescue us, we wait. Many of the patriarchs in the Bible had to wait. Abraham had to wait for the promised child. Isaac had to wait for his wife. Jacob had to wait to marry the love of his life.

The nation of Israel had to wait four hundred years in the captivity of Egypt before they were delivered. Moses had to endure forty years in the wilderness before he was ready to lead. Many years and many troubles separated David's anointing as king from the time he was a shepherd boy to the time when it was fulfilled.

So there is no question about it. Learning to wait on God is a bona fide sign of our sonship. There have been many, many times when I have cried out to Papa and asked Him how long I should wait, and He always replies with the same answer, "As long as it takes, son!"

My prayer is that the love of God would deal a deathblow to our adult-sized independent, self-sufficient egos. May God's goodness vanquish all suspicion that we have about our Father's motivations. May we all be able to come to the realization that we are not able to lead ourselves so we can embrace the beautiful simplicity of a life where we are led by the Spirit of God.

I had a real life example of this a few years ago when I had to speak at two different churches on the same Sunday morning. The churches were fifteen minutes apart by car and I only had fifteen minutes between each service. On top of that, both of the churches were located outside of the city where my GPS didn't work. Needless to say, I was a little stressed.

One of the elders saw that I was completely overwhelmed as she tried to give me directions to the next church. In her kindness, she offered to get in her car so I could follow her in my own car. Since I didn't have to pay attention to speed limits or approaching turns, I was able to enjoy the ride.

I can remember it was a beautiful fall day and the sun was glistening on the cornfields as we made our way through the countryside. At that moment, I didn't have a care in the world. I was simply enjoying the ride when I heard God say to me, "This is what it feels like to be led by My Spirit."

Boy, did I get what He was saying to me. If I am willing to do what I am told and nothing more or nothing less, I can live a life of rest and peace where I can simply enjoy where God is leading me.

The thing is though, if God isn't moving, we shouldn't be either. Think about the pillar of fire and the cloud that led the children of Israel in the wilderness. When the pillar wasn't moving, neither were the Israelites.

How many things are generated in our church life simply because we can't stand the tension of being still and waiting? May God give us all the wisdom to know when to move and when to stay.

The reality is, little kids are not charged with the responsibility of navigating the road maps on family trips. Their only responsibility is to have lots of fun in the back seat as mom and dad do all the driving. In the Kingdom of God, we are not charged with the responsibility of leading either. We simply follow.

Sure, leadership happens when God causes other people to follow us as we follow Him. In 1 Corinthians 11:1, Paul said,

"Follow me as I follow Christ." But, make no mistake about it, God is the One doing the leading. May we all embrace the beauty and wonderment that is ours when we simply allow ourselves to be led by the Spirit so that we can truly enjoy this ride we are on called *life*.

Isaiah 40:31
But those who wait for Yahweh will renew their strength. They will mount up with wings like eagles. They will run, and not be weary. They will walk, and not faint (WEB).

-22-
LITTLE CHILDREN LIVE FROM THEIR HEART

Over the years, I have had conversations with lots of folks who were trying to discern God's plan and purpose for their lives. It was as if they were searching for that elusive 'thing' that was part of their divine destiny they had not yet discovered.

Often during our conversation, I would ask them a very simple question, "What would you like to do?", at which many people have responded, "I don't know." I believe one of the reasons they struggle to live a fulfilled life is because they are disconnected from their own heart's desires.

Many people have grown up being so influenced by well-meaning parents, teachers and friends that they have never given themselves the permission to ask what it is they themselves want to do.

In some cultures, if you have strong academic abilities, the expectation is that you will become a doctor, a lawyer or some kind of professional, whether you like it or not. Add in the pressures from the media, the church and other authority figures, then things can get *really* confusing.

While there is wisdom in a multitude of counsellors (Proverbs 15:22), if we are not careful, we will completely rely on external influences to direct us. I believe God created us in such a way that our heart would be the compass that would help set the course of our life. It is the most precious thing we have been entrusted with. Our Heavenly Father considers our hearts to be very dear and worth guarding.

In 1 Samuel 16:7, God reminds the prophet Samuel that while most people make their judgements about a person based on their outward appearance, He sees into their heart. That is why Proverbs 4:23 tells us, "Above all else, guard your heart, for everything you do flows from it" (NIV).

The problem in many Christian circles is that we have a theology that portrays our hearts as vile and corrupt. Jeremiah 17:9 is often quoted to reinforce our belief that the heart is exceedingly wicked. "The heart is deceitful above all things, and it is exceedingly corrupt: who can know it?" (WEB).

If we embrace this kind of Old Covenant paradigm, we will most definitely not trust our heart. As a young Christian, I went as far as to make the assumption that God's will must be in direct opposition to my own heart's desires. As a result, I thought God would make me marry someone I didn't love, give me a ministry I didn't want and send me to a nation I didn't want to go to. Sounds crazy, huh?

If we think our hearts cannot be trusted, what do we look to in order to find direction? Unfortunately, we will be left looking to external influences like rules, regulations and other people's opinions and expectations to guide us.

If we are not careful, we may fall into a trap that is rooted in the fear of man, where we try to make everybody else happy and forget to consider what makes us happy. This will result in us living a life from our 'head' instead of living from our 'heart'.

But my question is, can our heart really be trusted? My answer to that is a resounding YES! Even in the Old Testament, there is a signpost pointing to a time when God would give us a new heart, which was fulfilled in the New Covenant.

Ezekiel 11:19-20
19 I will give them one heart, and I will put a new spirit within you; and I will take the stony heart out of their flesh, and will give them a heart of flesh; 20 that they may walk in my statutes, and keep my ordinances, and do them: and they shall be my people, and I will be their God (WEB).

And it is in this new heart that God pours out His love (Romans 5:5) that causes us to be rooted and grounded in His goodness (Ephesians 3:17). Now, everything has changed. In the Old Testament, the people had to rely on an external application of God's laws. But in the New Testament, we are directed and guided internally by our brand new heart.

1 John 2:27 says, "As for you, the anointing which you received from him remains in you, and you don't need for anyone to teach you. But as his anointing teaches you concerning all things, and is true, and is no lie, and even as it taught you, you will remain in him" (WEB).

What the Apostle John is saying here is that you can trust the indwelling Holy Spirit to guide you, and where does He dwell? ...in your heart! That is why the Apostle Paul writes in Philippians 2:13, "For it is God who works in you both to will and to work, for his good pleasure" (WEB).

I believe it takes faith to believe our heart can be trusted. Sure there is wisdom in hearing the counsel that comes from those around us, but I believe that ultimately, God intended our heart be in the driver's seat.

I have wrestled with this idea much of my Christian life. Having felt called into 'ministry' at the age of fifteen, I thought my only viable option would be to eventually end up in the role of a pastor. I did end up giving full time pastoring a go for a few years, but it never felt right. It was only when I was truly free to follow my heart that I ended up doing what I love to do and that involves sharing the good news of my Papa's love.

Little children are a beautiful example that we can all learn from. If a little child wants to do something, they do it. They don't think about doing it and they don't ask other people's opinion on whether to do it or not, they just do it. They live in an intuitive state where they simply follow their heart.

The older a child gets though, the more developed their awareness of other people's opinions are and the more their lives are shaped from external influences. No longer are they free to follow their heart. Now they have to consider so many other things that can eventually lead them to a place where they become disconnected from their own heart's desires.

I want to encourage you that your Heavenly Papa wants you to return to that place of simplicity of heart where you will be re-connected with your internal desires. For it is in your heart that God will direct you into His plans and purposes.

In the movie, *Chariots of Fire*, a man named Eric Liddle was a really good runner who competed for Great Britain in the 1924 Olympics. I so appreciate how he described his love for running with his love for God. He said, "God made me fast. And when I run, I feel His pleasure."

What are the things in your life where you feel the Father's pleasure? Take note of these things because that is how God is guiding you. He has placed His own Spirit within you, to cause you to desire the things He wants you to do so that you can fulfill the good works He has prepared for you before the foundation of the world (Ephesians 2:10).

God is not in opposition to the true desires of your heart. He put them there in the first place and He really enjoys seeing your heart's desires fulfilled. So take a deep breath, relax and ask Papa to show you your heart's desires.

Psalm 37:4
Take delight in the Lord, and he will give you the desires of your heart (WEB).

-23- LITTLE CHILDREN NEED TO BE COMFORTED

When our children fell and scraped their knee, they came searching for comfort. If they came to their dad, I tried to *fix* the problem and send them on their way. If I was their only option, I would suffice. But if their mom was close by, she was always their first choice.

Sometimes they wouldn't even be crying until they locked eyes with their mom, at which point they would burst into tears running into her arms. The kids weren't looking for a fix to their owie; they were looking for comfort. And if comfort was what they sought, their mom would provide all of the comfort they needed.

Little children need to be comforted and they make no apology for it. As they get older though, their need for comfort doesn't change, but their pursuit of it does.

By the time they become adults, the vulnerable little boy or girl gives way to a hardened shell of a man or woman who doesn't appear to need comfort...but they still do.

There is little room in our society for adults to receive the comfort they truly need. After all, acknowledging we need it would require vulnerability and an open heartedness that is no longer safe for big people to express. So what do we do? We still seek out comfort, but since parental comfort is no longer an option, we have to find it in counterfeit places.

Maybe we will find it in the refrigerator? Isn't it funny that certain kinds of foods are even called *comfort food*? Maybe we will find comfort in a relationship? Or maybe in an addiction? Make no mistake, we were all created by God to need comfort and we will seek it out whether we are two or one hundred and two.

The wonderful thing about true comfort is that it actually brings a peace and security that calms our soul. True comfort restores us to a place of rest and safety. While we may still be hurting, somehow comfort provides us with warmth and an assurance that everything will be all right.

False comfort on the other hand, provides no real assurance in the deepest part of our being. It leads us on a never-ending quest to fill a void that can never be filled by these counterfeit affections.

No wonder our society is experiencing so many problems today. There are entire industries that have been created to provide a buffet of false comforts which only fan into flame our insatiable appetites and lead to even greater indulgences, leaving us empty again.

In 2 Corinthians 1:3-4 Paul writes:
3 Praise be to the God and Father of our Lord Jesus Christ, the Father of compassion and the God of all comfort, 4 who comforts us in all our troubles, so that we can comfort those in any trouble with the comfort we ourselves receive from God (NIV).

God is the Father of compassion and the God of ALL comfort. He is the source of all the comfort we need. If we would just realize this, we could turn to Him and truly be consoled. The amazing thing is, when we really receive comfort from God, we are able to comfort others in the same way He has imparted it to us.

So what prevents us from going to God for comfort? Well, I think the first thing is society teaches us that when we grow up, we don't need comfort any longer. Have you ever heard the expression, *Big boys don't cry*?

From an early age, in our effort to toughen up our children to prepare them for the harsh realities of the world, we encourage them to close off their need for comfort. It actually doesn't work because we were created to need comfort, so all we do is mask this need and pretend it no longer exists.

So that is why it is so important for us to return to that place of childlike vulnerability towards God. When we are aware that we still need to be comforted, we are more likely to position our hearts to receive it in the times we need it.

I have been learning a thing or two about comfort in this past year. When our youngest daughter, Candice, was diagnosed with Leukemia at twenty-five years of age, everything within me was rocked to the core. In the early days of her diagnosis, I felt like my emotions were on autopilot so I could be strong for the entire family.

I remember on one of my nightly walks from the hospital to my car, I was feeling all alone and I said to God, "Where are you? I can't hear your voice." To be honest, I wasn't feeling a great sense of peace, as I was doing everything I could to just hold it all together.

I didn't hear God's voice, so I wondered where He was. Right then, Papa gave me a sense of where He was. He was walking right alongside of me, arm in arm, but He was completely silent. He wasn't correcting me for my disengaged emotions. He wasn't rebuking me for not feeling at peace, He was just silent.

And in that moment of silence, I realized He was suffering alongside of me. As the perfect Father, He understood like no one else how much I was suffering alongside of my own daughter. In the darkness, walking all alone, right at that very moment, I received a profound sense of God's comfort.

Not only does He comfort us with the paternal love of a father, He comforts us with the maternal love of a mother as well. In Isaiah 66:13, we read about this when God speaks of His heart for Israel. "As a mother comforts her child, so will I comfort you; and you will be comforted over Jerusalem" (NIV).

This past eighteen months has awakened me to what it means that God is called the Father of compassion. In Psalm 103:13-14, King David describes God's compassionate heart: 13 As a father has compassion on his children, so the Lord has compassion on those who fear him; 14 for he knows how we are formed, he remembers that we are dust (NIV).

The Latin word for compassion means '*to suffer together*'. If God is truly the Father of compassion, it stands to reason that He is suffering alongside every person on the planet in the midst of their trials. The very idea that He is so connected to those He loves in this intimate way absolutely blows every circuit in my brain.

And yet, most of us continue to suffer unaware of His nearness. My prayer is that you would be awakened to your own need to be comforted by God and His closeness to you. Psalm 34:18

says, "Yahweh is near to those who have a broken heart, and saves those who have a crushed spirit" (WEB).

Just like a little child runs into the loving arms of their parent when they need to be consoled, may you find a new freedom to run into the big, strong arms of your Heavenly Dad and experience the love and peace His comfort brings.

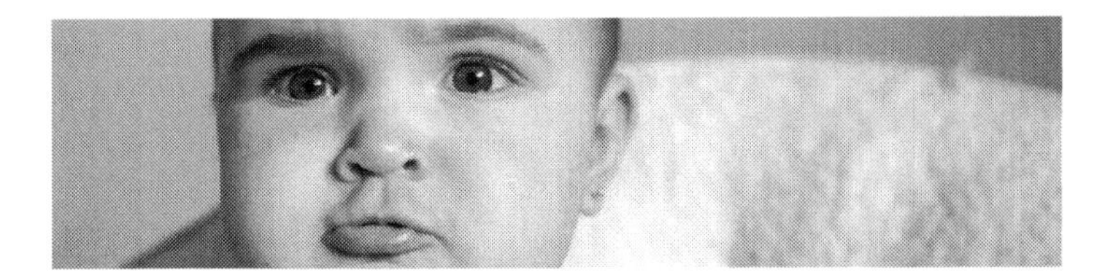

-24-
LITTLE CHILDREN RESPOND TO DISCIPLINE

When my children were little, I never enjoyed the times when I had to discipline them. I preferred those moments to be replaced with play times, as that was much easier. But the reality is, my correction was as much a demonstration of my love as my cuddles were.

There is a common expression where a parent is about to discipline their child and before they do, they say, "This is going to hurt me more than it is going to hurt you." From the child's perspective, this couldn't be further from the truth. But if you are a loving parent, you know how true these words are.

It is never easy to bring correction and I am thinking it never should be easy. If it did become easy, I would question the heart of the one who is doing the correcting. Nevertheless, disciplining our children is a very important cog in the wheel of their development.

When my little chickadees ran into my arms crying after they were disciplined, it absolutely rocked me to the core. Adults tend to run away when they are hurt, but little kids who know they need to be comforted, run directly into the arms of the one who just disciplined them.

Hebrews 12 has a lot to say about how God disciplines His children. Verse 7 says, "It is for discipline that you endure. God deals with you as with children, for what son is there whom his father doesn't discipline" (WEB)?

There is not much talk about the Father's discipline in church circles. I can't imagine even one person signing up to a conference that would focus on being disciplined. I think the reason we have such an aversion to this is because we confuse the word *discipline* with our own experiences of being punished in an ungodly way.

The root word for discipline is the same as the word *disciple*. God is training up His kids to grow in their sonship and He always has our best interests at heart. If a stove is hot, we serve our children well by teaching them not to touch the stove or they will be burnt. The motivation behind the training is ultimately for their protection.

Being disciplined isn't a pleasant experience but the end result is what the parent is after. Hebrews 12:11 says it this way, "All chastening seems for the present to be not joyous but grievous; yet afterward it yields the peaceful fruit of righteousness to those who have been exercised thereby" (WEB).

Oftentimes, we mistakenly think God's discipline is actually an unloving form of punishment because of how we were disciplined by our own parents. Thankfully, I didn't receive many spankings as a child, but in reality I didn't need to. One disapproving look from my father would devastate me.

Because my dad struggled with anger in my early years, I was afraid to do anything that would cause his anger to be focused on me. So part of the journey of me being able to respond to my Heavenly Father's loving discipline is to realize His motivation is not anger, but love.

For some people, their experience with parental discipline might have resulted in shame. A common expression that parents would say to their children when I was growing up was, *Shame on you*! Think about that statement for a moment. Shame goes beyond saying you have done a bad action. Shame says you are a bad person.

I am so thankful our Heavenly Father has no interest in shaming us. As a matter of fact, He takes away all of our shame and replaces it with a double portion of His own goodness. That is what it says in Isaiah 61:7: Instead of your shame you will receive a double portion, and instead of disgrace you will rejoice in your inheritance. And so you will inherit a double portion in your land, and everlasting joy will be yours (NIV).

My prayer is that you would not be afraid of your Heavenly Father's discipline. He is not angry with you, He is not disappointed in you and He has absolutely no interest in hurting you. He is training you up as His beloved son or daughter and His discipline is a part of that process.

I can remember a time when I was twenty years of age, I was about to make a very unwise decision to visit a neighbor's house to see if I could buy some marijuana. I had been a Christian for five years at this point and was completely free from my past life, which involved such things.

However, in the spur of the moment, I thought it might be fun to revisit my (not so good) past for at least one day and buy a joint. I put on my clogs (wooden platform sandals), took one step out of my house and twisted my ankle, which stopped me in my tracks.

I went back into my house and ended up at the emergency room where I discovered I had broken my foot. When I got back into my car to drive home, I was overwhelmed with the sense of God's love as I realized God, in His mercy, prevented me from making a very poor choice that day.

I'm not saying He caused my foot to be broken, but He definitely used that experience to train me up as a son and keep me from doing something that was really stupid.

On that note, I think it is important for me to say that I do not believe that God disciplines us with calamities and disease. He is a good Father who gives good gifts to His children. It would simply not be consistent for God to use the same tactics the devil uses.

In John 10:10, we see a contrast between the thief and the Son. "The thief's purpose is to steal and kill and destroy. My purpose is to give them a rich and satisfying life (NLT)."

However, since we live in a fallen world, there are ripple effects that touch each one of us. While all things in our lives are not good, our Father's great love will cause all things to work together for our good in the end (Romans 8:28).

So be encouraged and comforted knowing there is a harvest of righteousness awaiting every son and daughter who has been trained up in the way they should go. May we all have the tenderness and humility of a little child who runs into the arms of our Father when we experience His loving discipline.

Hebrews 12:10
For our earthly fathers disciplined us for a few years, doing the best they knew how. But God's discipline is always good for us, so that we might share in his holiness (NLT).

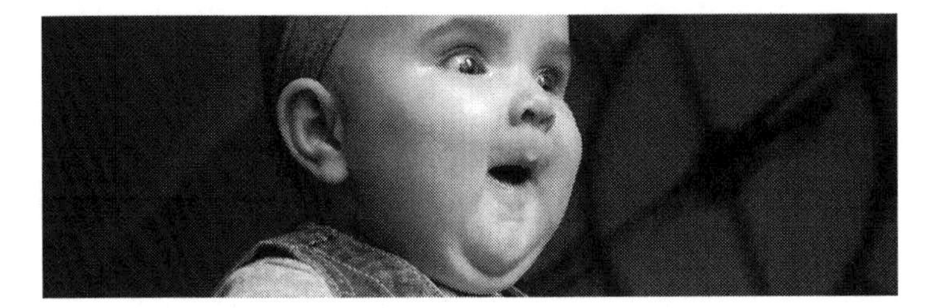

-25-
LITTLE CHILDREN ARE CURIOUS

There is a beautiful curiosity that little children exhibit as they comprehend the wonders around them. Our little Riley is at a stage in her life where every empty box represents something new to explore. I think it is funny that often, the packaging is more interesting to her than the toy contained within it!

Every new thing she discovers is amazing to her. There is so much to be discovered that sometimes you can see her almost explode with excitement. With every new encounter, more information is being stored in her little brain. It is a beautiful thing to behold.

I can remember when my own children were at the stage where they asked questions nonstop. "What is that? What is that? What is that?" Every new thing had to be explained to them in a way they could grasp.

But then they added the question *Why?* to every *What?* question, which made the answer a whole lot more complicated to try and explain. Often, as a result of the nonstop barrage of *Why?* questions, my only answer would be, "Just because."

Any parent can attest to the fact that this hunger for input and information can drive you a little crazy, but it is still a beautiful thing to behold. You don't have to teach a child to be inquisitive; they just are because that is how God made them. In the eyes of a little child, the world is a very exciting place to live.

Every moment of every day presents a new opportunity for them to learn and grow some more. They are not concerned in the least what people think of their hunger for new experiences because they are completely wrapped up in each encounter as it comes.

I kind of think this open hearted curiosity to experience new things might be what Jesus was talking about in the Sermon on the Mount in Matthew 5:6 when He said, "Blessed are those who hunger and thirst after righteousness, for they shall be filled"(WEB).

I realize Jesus was talking about spiritual hunger for the things of God, but it is the *hunger* and *thirst* I find interesting. In order to be hungry or thirsty, we must first have a tangible need for food or water. If we don't have a need, we won't have the desire.

Over the years, I have discovered that the easiest places for me to minister are places where the room is filled with spiritually hungry people. It is as if these dear folks pull the anointing of God right out of me with very little effort on my part, so it is a very fun environment for me to be in.

There have been times when I have shared the same message that has been received really well with a bunch of hungry and thirsty folk, to dear people who were not as interested or engaged in what I was sharing. Instead of my mouth trying to catch up with the overflow of my heart, I felt like I was trudging through a waist high field of resistance.

In the early days of my teaching, it was easy for me to beat myself up after these kind of meetings because I thought I did something wrong. After all, I thought, if I didn't make a significant connection with them, I must have been at fault.

But one day, Papa spoke to me after one of those kinds of meetings and said, "Barry, relax. You are the same in these meetings as you are in the other ones. The people are just not hungry. So if they aren't hungry, they won't eat, no matter how much food you give them."

These words of encouragement helped me understand a really important principle in the Kingdom. Whether we call it *spiritual hunger* or at times *desperation for God* or even *curiosity*, it is all the same. When our hearts are open to experience new things, we are in a position of humility where we can receive.

If we are stuffed full and have no interest in receiving anything else, we will not position ourselves to feast at the buffet that is set before us. In Revelation 3:14-22, we read of Jesus' word to the church at Laodicea. There is no question that it is a tough word for them to swallow because Jesus strikes at the very heart of their apathy.

He told them that though they thought they were rich, in reality, they were poor. Though they thought they were clothed, in fact, they were naked. Though they thought they could see, the harsh truth was that they were blind. In a nutshell, they thought they were *in need of nothing.*

When we are in a place where we think we've got it all and have no need, we will close ourselves off to anything new God wants to give us. It is in this place of complacency that the Kingdom of God loses its luster and wonder to us, whereas little kids are always hungry and thirsty for new experiences and encounters.

Their little lives are not marred with pride so they are over the moon excited to learn and experience new things. They are not embarrassed about their interest in learning and they do not pretend to know more than they do. They are just open to as much as they can receive.

I want to be like that. I want to be in a place where I never stop receiving and experiencing the good things Papa has prepared for me. One of the desires in my own heart is that the wonder of God's love would never get old to me. I never want to be in a place where I become so professional at ministering the Father's love that I cease to be a little boy with a BIG Dad.

There is an expression that sums up adult sized cynicism, "Been there, done that, bought the t-shirt." I don't ever want to be in a place where I close my heart off to fresh new encounters, even if they are hidden in the familiar.

As crazy as it might sound, one of the greatest obstacles to receiving a deeper revelation of the Father's love is the *message* of the Father's love. This might sound like a weird thing for me to say, but let me explain by giving this example:

If I want to be protected from getting the flu, I will get a flu shot. From what I understand of this process, the needle contains a tiny little bit of the flu virus to help my own immune system build up a resistance to the flu. So when the flu comes knocking, my body has the ability to resist it.

In the same way, if we receive a little bit of information about God's love for us, we can assume we have something we do not yet have. This can result in us becoming inoculated from a deeper revelation of God's love because we have attained a knowledge of His goodness without coming into an experiential reality of it.

If you've experienced God loving you through a conference, a book or a time of prayer ministry, that's great, but I want to encourage you to keep your heart open for more just like little kids do.

I can remember going to a church in another country where the well-meaning pastor told me he had already heard the Father's love message from all the main speakers. He asked me, "What else do you have?" I'm not sure how I answered him, but in my heart, I wanted to scream out loud, "What else is there?"

My prayer is that the revelation that Almighty God is our Dad would be as new and fresh today as it was the day we first received it. I pray we would all embrace the childlike curiosity and open hearted hunger to taste and see the goodness of God (Psalm 34:8) at every opportunity.

Since God's mercies are new every morning (Lamentations 3:22-23), every day is a fresh, new opportunity to experience God like we have never experienced Him before. As we continue to behold the Lord's face as in a mirror, may our curiosity and childlike awe and wonder transport us from one degree of glory to the next.

2 Corinthians 3:18
But we all, with unveiled face seeing the glory of the Lord as in a mirror, are transformed into the same image from glory to glory, even as from the Lord, the Spirit (WEB).

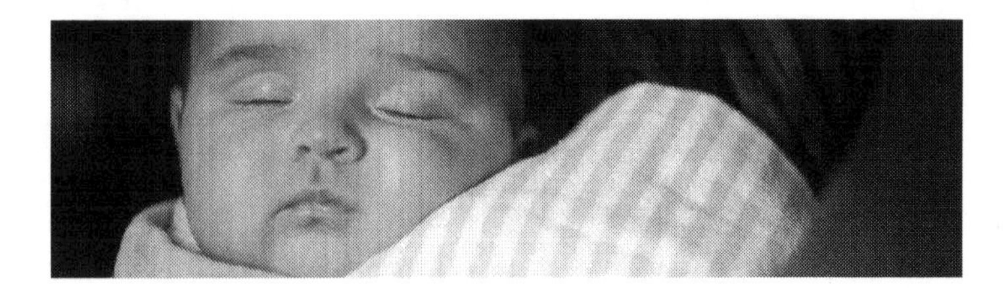

-26-
LITTLE CHILDREN ARE CONTENT

There are often values in the Kingdom that appear as paradoxes and yet they work hand in hand with each other. I just finished writing about the importance of having childlike hunger and now I am going to write about living in a state of childlike contentment.

How can you be hungry and content at the same time? Is it even possible? I think the answer is *yes*. Even when we are spiritually hungry, we still have all we need in that moment. While spiritual hunger and thirst are intended to keep our hearts in a receiving mode, God wants us to be content in whatever state we are in.

Make no mistake about it though, there is a promise of being filled for every person that is hungry for righteousness and that infilling is incredibly satisfying. I believe we can live in a state of being completely satisfied and yet open to more all at the same time.

I think this is a tension that requires the help of the Holy Spirit to navigate through. But like so much else in the Kingdom, we cannot reconcile these things through an adult mindset. After all, how can we be weak and strong at the same time? Poor and rich? So, may God give you the wisdom to help you reconcile how this can work for you.

One of the awesome characteristics of a revival culture is the hunger for more. When we realize we have not yet arrived, our humble heart is ready to receive more of what our Papa has for us. The thing that might not be so good is if we are in such a state of pursuing what we do not yet have, we become restless.

While I am all for the greater things that are yet to come, may our spiritual pursuits not rob us of the beautiful, serene contentment that peace brings to our heart right now. The Apostle Paul wrote about the secret of being content in Philippians 4:11-13 when he said, "for I have learned in whatever state I am, to be content in it" (WEB).

King David knew a thing or two about ruling from a place of childlike contentment when he penned Psalm 131:1-2: 1 My heart is not proud, Lord, my eyes are not haughty; I do not concern myself with great matters or things too wonderful for me. 2 But I have calmed and quieted myself, I am like a weaned child with its mother; like a weaned child I am content (NIV).

This picture David paints is one of the best examples in the Bible of how we can rule our own kingdom with the heart of a child. There is no better picture of complete satisfaction I have ever seen than seeing our little Riley after she had just had her complete fill of her mother's milk.

Being completely stuffed to the max of all the love and nourishment her mom could give her, she is free to drift off into the deepest of sleeps while still in her mom's arms. That is contentment at its best. Fully satisfied and fully at peace in the safety of the arms of love.

Notice David writes that he doesn't concern himself with great matters or things beyond his pay grade. The Amplified Bible translates it this way, "I don't concern myself with matters too great or too awesome for me to grasp" (AMP). Charles Spurgeon wrote about this passage of Scripture in his Spurgeon's Verse Expositions of the Bible: "High things may suit others who are of greater stature, and yet they may be quite unfit for us. A man does well to know his own size."[6]

I believe one of the secrets to living a contented life is not to overreach. I've heard it said that when we overreach, we are trying to boil the ocean rather than the pot we have been entrusted with. But herein lies another paradox.

Jesus told us we do would greater things than He did because He was going to be with the Father (John 14:12). Since Jesus did some really great things, greater things must be really, really great. And often, these great things require risk, stretching and lots of faith.

So in a Christian culture that is always moving towards the 'greater things', we need to be mindful not to sacrifice our personal contentment in the process. Spiritual hunger is absolutely essential, but there is a huge difference between being genuinely passionate for more of God and just being restless.

I think it is wise to remember that anything in your life, whether good or bad, that causes you to lose your peace is not from God. 2 Thessalonians 3:16 says, "Now may the Lord of peace himself give you peace at all times in all ways. The Lord be with you all" (WEB). God wants you to be at peace at ALL times and in EVERY way!

If our value to God is based on our ability to change in order to finally become loveable, we will not be able to rest in the love that He is loving us with right now. This is one of the great lies the enemy of our soul wants us to believe.

A while back, I was teaching a school of young hungry hearts when I opened the class up to questions. One of these young students asked me a question I had never been asked before. She asked, "If you could share one thing with us that you have learned as you have grown in the revelation of God's love, what would it be?"

Without giving any thought to my answer, I responded by saying, "The thing I have learned and am continuing to learn is that I am loved completely by God the way that I am and I am enough."

When I said the words "I am enough," I felt a tangible sense of God's presence settle on the room as I realized how important this was to me personally and to the cry of the human heart. I prayed for everyone in the room that they would know their Heavenly Father loves them completely and that their lives were enough.

Little children have no concept of feeling inadequate. They are who they are and they do not even have the capacity to doubt whether they are enough or not. It is only when they grow up that ungodly measurements and comparisons erode the tangible peace contentment brings.

May God give you the grace to know from the very core of your being, that you are completely and fully loved and that your life is enough. May you be so filled with El Shaddai's (The Many Breasted One) nurturing love, that you will be fully satisfied with who you are in His sight, so that you will be able to drift off to sleep in His big, strong arms.

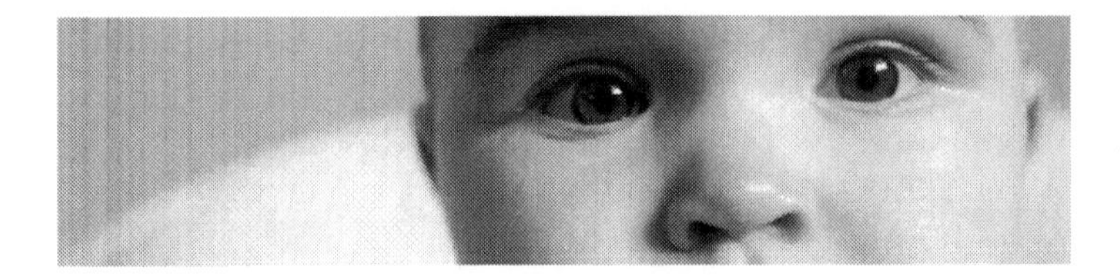

-27-
LITTLE CHILDREN ARE INNOCENT

The best example of innocence we can find on this planet can be found in the face of a little child. If you look into their eyes, you will not see any guile, falsehood, or anything unlovely. What you will see is authenticity and complete innocence.

When Jesus sent His disciples out, He told them to be wise as serpents yet as innocent as doves (Matthew 10:16). I believe the innocence Jesus referred to is part and parcel of what qualifies little children for true greatness in the Kingdom.

As I mentioned earlier in the book, I'm not trying to negate the fact that every person is born with a sin nature. We sin because we are sinners, not the other way around. So we all need a Savior. But there is no disputing the fact that little babies come into this world with an innocence that is theirs by God's design.

As little babies, they have no conscience to guide them, good or bad. They have no knowledge of good and they have no knowledge of evil. They just are who they are.

Is there anywhere in the Bible where we see this kind of innocence displayed? If you guessed the Garden of Eden pre-fall, you would be right. Just like babies do today, Adam and

Eve ran in the garden completely oblivious to the fact they had no clothes on. They were completely innocent of sin and without shame.

Only when they ate from the wrong tree did they become aware of both good and evil. When Adam and Eve ate the fruit that came from the Tree of Knowledge of Good and Evil, they lost their innocence. A part of them died that day.

There is an interesting passage in Romans 7:9 where Paul makes a very provocative statement. "I was alive apart from the law once, but when the commandment came, sin revived, and I died" (WEB).

Some commentaries interpret this to mean that Paul was referring to a time of childlike innocence but other commentaries say he was referring to a time in his Pharisaical arrogance where he thought he was justified based on his own works.

Though I am not a theologian of any kind, I tend to lean towards the school of thought that Paul was referring to his time of childlike innocence. As far as I am concerned, this makes the most sense.

According to Jewish customs, a child is free from observing the law prior to their bar mitzvah celebration, which happens when they become a teenager. The words *bar mitzvah* literally mean *son of the commandment.* From age zero to thirteen, they are in a sense, free from the law that is entrusted to them at their celebration of manhood.

So, if Paul was referring to his time of childlike innocence, which were his pre-law days, it is helpful for us to understand why the attribute of returning to childlike innocence can serve us so well today. While the spirit of the law is good, having the responsibility to continually discern good from evil is a burden God never intended His kids to bear.

Prior to eating from The Tree of Knowledge of Good and Evil, humanity's first couple had nothing in them that was self-conscience of right and wrong. They simply lived their lives knowing they were completely loved and accepted just as they were.

But when they ate from the wrong tree, all of a sudden, their innocence was replaced with a new found knowledge that had devastating consequences. We read about this in Genesis 3:9-11 when God is looking for them to walk with Him in the cool of the day.

9 Yahweh God called to the man, and said to him, "Where are you?" 10 The man said, "I heard your voice in the garden, and I was afraid, because I was naked; and I hid myself." 11 God said, "Who told you that you were naked? Have you eaten from the tree that I commanded you not to eat from" (WEB)?

It is the "Who told you that you were naked?" loss of innocence that Jesus came to restore in the New Covenant. In the life of every child, we can see a shadow of the beautiful innocence that can be ours once again through the finished work of the cross.

When kids are little, their parents are like God to them. Everything they receive is from their parents. Their parents tell them who they are and what they are capable of. Whether good or bad, their view of themselves and the world around them are shaped by their experience of family love.

That is why you will often find little children boasting about their parents. 'My mommy is the most beautiful mommy in the world!' 'My daddy is the strongest daddy ever!', and the one

I think is absolutely hilarious... 'My dad can beat up your dad!' Sadly, something happens: little children grow up and they see their parents differently.

One of the tragedies every child experiences along the way is the loss of their innocence. Unfortunately, for many children, it happens far earlier than God intended. As a child, I can remember thinking my family life was completely normal. I assumed our family was just like every other family in the neighborhood.

It was only when I began to spend time at other friends' houses that I realized my dad's overuse of alcohol wasn't considered normal in other families. The moment I realized that, another part of my innocence was lost.

Regrettably, today more than ever, we are seeing the loss of our childlike innocence earlier and earlier. Today, little kids are being bombarded by things in the media and on the Internet that they should never see. Add to that a broken educational system that is forcing them to learn things they should never have to learn. This is not how our Father intended for little kids to live.

But the good news is that through what Jesus Christ did on the cross, we have our innocence restored. Isaiah 1:18 says, though our sins are as scarlet, they will be made white as wool. Hebrews 8:12 tells us that God forgives and He forgets our sin.

Romans 8:33 says, "Who could bring a charge against God's chosen ones? It is God who justifies" (WEB). I love the definition of the word 'justify' that describes it as 'Just-if-I'd-never-sinned!' I truly believe God has restored us to a place in His eyes that He sees us as if we have never sinned. That is the restoration of innocence in all its glory.

I am convinced there is a safe place in the heart of our Heavenly Father where we no longer have to live a life preoccupied with right and wrong. I believe there is a place of childlike innocence where we are free to live from our hearts, oblivious to the shame and condemnation that the Tree of Knowledge of Good and Evil can bring.

Little kids live in this place of innocence intuitively and without apology. May we live there too, knowing our God and Father has declared us righteous because of the finished work of the cross (2 Corinthians 5:21).

May you find the grace to return to the place of childlike innocence, where you can boldly declare to the people around you that your Heavenly Dad really is the biggest, best Dad in the entire universe.

Jude 1:24-25
24 Now to him who is able to keep them from stumbling, and to present you faultless before the presence of his glory in great joy, 25 to God our Savior, who alone is wise, be glory and majesty, dominion and power, both now and forever. Amen (WEB).

-28-
LITTLE CHILDREN LIVE IN THE MOMENT

Little babies have absolutely no concept of the past or the future. They simply live in each moment as it comes. As a child grasps concepts about time, they can differentiate the present from the future by simple measurements.

I remember when our children were little, we would try and help them understand future events by measuring days by the number of sleeps left. We'd say, "We are going to grandma's house in two sleeps" or "We are going on vacation in five sleeps from now."

Even when little kids grasp the concept of past, present and future, it is always a joy to watch them choose to live their little lives full on in the present. I believe this is a gift God has given them and one many that adults have lost the ability to do along the way.

In the adult world we live in, many people find it difficult to stay in the present. Our tendency is to spend much of our time being distracted by things that have happened in the past or things that may happen in the future.

Children have no such distractions. They have a God given

ability to stay in the moment and live each moment to the fullest. Could you imagine how you would feel if you saw your two year old obsessing about world events? Or how about if they were living in regret because of an untimely outburst they had a few days ago?

It sounds ludicrous to even believe little kids would have the capacity to think of such things. However, as adults, we can live so much in the past that we allow it to negatively influence our present. The same goes for the future.

I've heard it said that 75% of the things we worry about never come to pass. If that is the case, worry is a complete waste of time. It is like adults are willing to spend an incredible amount of time thinking about things that will never happen. Yet, many of us invest much of our present worrying about the future.

Have you ever been involved in a conversation where you felt the other person wasn't fully engaged with you? Perhaps they were looking over your shoulder trying to spot the next person they wanted to talk with? Or maybe you could see they were thinking about something else as you were sharing your heart with them? How did that make you feel? Pretty lousy, huh?

On the other hand, how do you feel when you are in a conversation with someone who is fully engaged with what you are saying? It feels really nice to be with someone who is not distracted by the past or the future, and has decided to be wholeheartedly with you in the now.

That is how God is. Psalm 46:1 says, "God is our refuge and strength, a very present help in trouble" (WEB). Did you catch that? He is *a very present help*, which means He is with you right now. When Moses asked God to tell him His name, God responded by saying, *I AM WHO I AM* (Exodus 3:13-14).

Though Jesus is called the Alpha and the Omega (the beginning and the end), He is not called the *I was* or the *I will be*. The Triune God is always in the present tense as the Great I AM.

The strategy of the enemy is to kill, steal and destroy (John 10:10). One of the ways he attempts to do this is by luring us out of the present where God dwells, so we would either live in the past or obsess about the future.

In reality, both of these dimensions of time are beyond our control. We cannot change the past and we cannot predict the future. If the enemy can convince us to make our dwelling place in either time zone, we will in fact, miss the moment by moment choices that we can influence in the present.

Think of it this way: If I spend half my time beating myself up for not exercising yesterday, and the other half of my time worrying about whether I will have time to exercise tomorrow, I will have no time left to exercise today. God loves it when we live in the moment just like little kids do.

I love watching our granddaughter literally squeeze every ounce of enjoyment out of each minute she is awake. I am so thankful she is with me through and through when we are experiencing our many adventures together.

My prayer is that you would be freed from everything in your past so you can live in the moment. I am so glad our God and Father forgives and forgets (Hebrews 8:12). The Apostle Paul had a pretty checkered past but he chose to forget what was in his past.

Philippians 3:13-14
Brothers, I don't regard myself as yet having taken hold, but one thing I do. Forgetting the things which are behind, and

stretching forward to the things which are before, 14 I press on towards the goal for the prize of the high calling of God in Christ Jesus (WEB).

I also pray you would be freed from worrying about your future. Jesus told us in Matthew 6:27 that worrying is an exercise in futility when He said, "Which of you, by being anxious, can add one moment to his lifespan?" (WEB)

In the previous verse, Jesus tells His disciples that the reason they need not worry is because they have a Heavenly Father who has promised to look after them. Verse 26 says, "See the birds of the sky, that they don't sow, neither do they reap, nor gather into barns. Your heavenly Father feeds them. Aren't you of much more value than they?" (WEB)

So my reminder to you is that God has forgiven your past and He has already secured your future so you could live in this very moment with Him. May God give you the grace to return to the beautiful simplicity of a little child who enjoys every moment as it comes.

Brother Lawrence described living in the moment really well when he said, "There is not in the world a kind of life more sweet and delightful than that of continual conversation with God."[7]

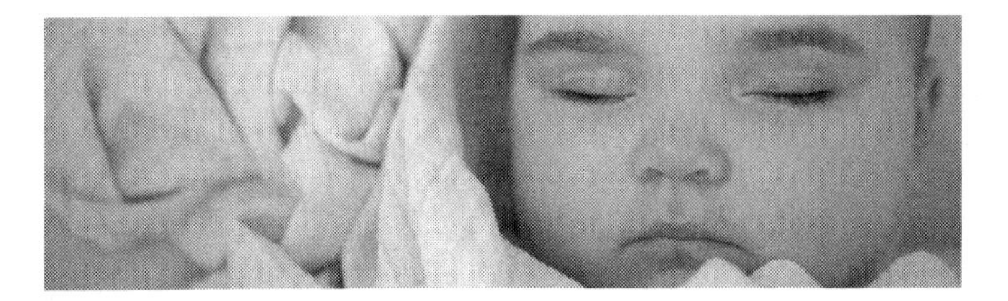

-29-
LITTLE CHILDREN LIKE SECURITY BLANKETS

Our granddaughter has a very special pink blanket that goes wherever she goes. This security blanket is her closest companion. The embroidered words 'Jesus loves me' lets everybody in Riley's space know whom she belongs to.

Recently, my wife and I went for a walk with Riley to test out the new stroller we bought her. We brought her little pink lamb blanket along for the ride so she could give it a comforting squeeze whenever she wanted to.

She kept throwing the blanket onto the sidewalk causing us to stop every so often to retrieve it and restore it back to its rightful owner. I kind of think this became a little a game for our dear Riley. When we got back to our house, we realized the much loved security blanket was gone.

In a bit of a panic, I retraced our steps so I could find it again. I was quite concerned because I knew just how special this little blanket was to Riley. My heart was pounding; I knew the children were going to be let out of school soon and if one of them found the blanket before I did, it would probably find a new home.

It was such a relief for me when I caught a glimpse of the little pink lump of cloth, basking in the sunlight on the sidewalk about a mile away from our home. At that moment, I heard the Lord speak to me about the role security blankets have in our lives.

Security blankets are meant to provide a little child with comfort, warmth, and a sense of familiarity that will reassure them even when they are in unfamiliar places. While it is appropriate for a little child to drag it around wherever they go, there comes a time when they have to leave it behind in order to go to school.

I felt Papa say to me that oftentimes, as adults we have security blankets that provide us with comfort and a sense of safety too. While there will come a time when we will have to leave them behind just like little kids do, our Heavenly Father is not threatened by them in the least.

As a matter of fact, He invites us to bring our security blanket (or insecurity blanket) with us right into His heart. He won't try to yank it out of our hand prematurely, but will patiently love us until we are ready to let it go ourselves.

My prayer is that you would know that God understands you like no one ever could. He knows why you hold onto things that provide false comfort and He sees the day when you will be finally free from these counterfeit affections. But even when you are clutching onto things that only provide temporary comfort, He will never stop loving you.

He is a good Father who carries you close to His heart on both your good days and your bad days. His love will never change even when you are hanging onto your insecurity blanket for dear life.

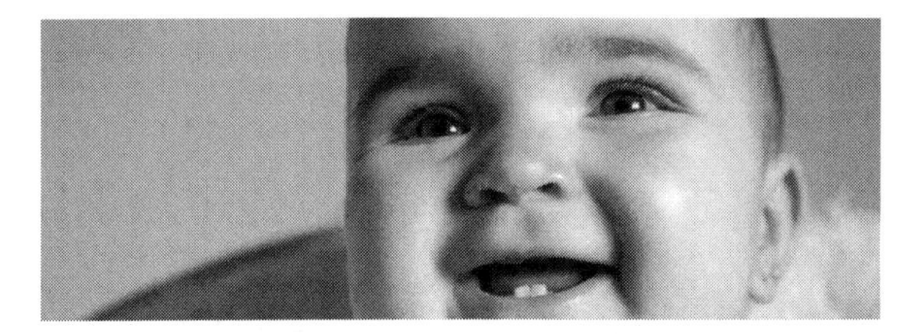

-30-
LITTLE CHILDREN FORGIVE EASILY

It was interesting to watch our children interact with each other when they were little. One minute they could be playing wonderfully together and the next minute they could be having a larger than life conflict. It may have taken an adult to intervene, but before long, they were playing and laughing together again as if nothing had ever happened.

Since little kids are authentic and transparent, you will not see them trying to veil their feelings. They are who they are, so when they are hurt, the whole world around them will see it in all its glory. However, they also have an amazing ability to forgive and forget that big people could really benefit from.

In the adult world we live in, we struggle to forgive. We hold onto offences much longer than we should, and the result is that it takes a heavy toll on our lives. I have seen firsthand the devastation unforgiveness brings to a family.

My dad's mother came from a Scottish family that was known for their tendency to hold grudges. It was as if there was no room for mistakes and very little grace to forgive and forget any offences that were committed. Unfortunately, the result was a very fractured family filled with broken relationships.

My grandmother ended up disowning my dad, which caused a pain in his heart that he never got over. I can remember him sending her flowers and cards on every special occasion and each gift went unanswered. Not only did my dad miss out on having a mom, but his mom missed out on being a mother and a grandmother.

My friend Jack Winter used to say, “Bitterness is a poison pill that we swallow thinking it will kill someone else.” While we may think we are getting a measure of justice by holding people accountable for their actions, in reality, it is us who are imprisoned.

There is no question that forgiveness is giving a person a gift they don’t deserve. In Matthew 18:21-35, Peter asked Jesus how many times he should forgive his brother. Jesus answered by telling a story about a king and a servant who owed him lots of money.

After realizing the servant was unable to pay back the debt he owed, the king had compassion on him and forgave the debt. When this same servant had the opportunity to forgive someone who only owed him just a little bit of money, he had no compassion and refused to forgive. The story ends with the man being thrown into a prison of his own making because of his inability to forgive others, even though he was forgiven himself.

If we can learn from the way little children interact with each other, maybe we can be able to forgive and forget too. Little kids have short memories for offences, whereas adults can hold onto grudges for years. From my own personal experience, I remember how amazed I was when my own children were so willing to forgive me when I blew it. If they acted like adults when they were small, it could have taken a long time to repair what they were willing to forgive in an instant.

The Apostle Paul begins Ephesians 4 with these words:
1 I therefore, the prisoner in the Lord, beg you to walk worthily of the calling with which you were called, 2 with all lowliness and humility, with patience, bearing with one another in love; 3 being eager to keep the unity of the Spirit in the bond of peace (WEB).

He ends the chapter by giving us a charge to be tenderhearted with one another: 31 Let all bitterness, wrath, anger, outcry, and slander, be put away from you, with all malice. 32 And be kind to one another, tender hearted, forgiving each other, just as God also in Christ forgave you (WEB).

There are no more tenderhearted people on this planet than little kids. If love keeps no record of wrongs as 1 Corinthians 13:5 tells us, then little children are a beautiful expression of love here on earth.

May we all learn how to grow up by growing down. May we be little again, and quick to forgive, so we can be authentic in the way we relate to each other… just like little kids do.

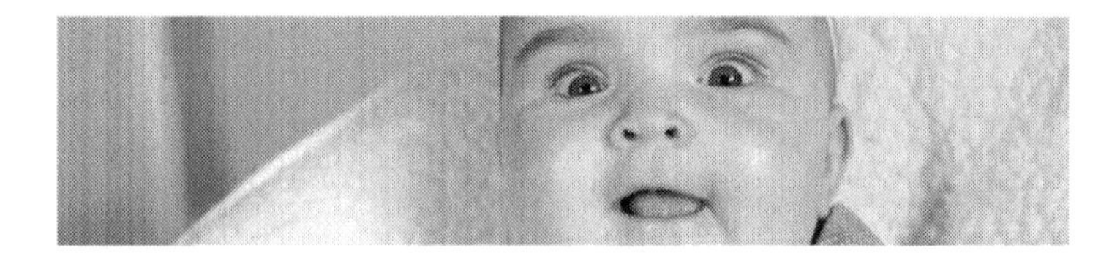

-31-
LITTLE CHILDREN ARE AUTHENTIC

Little children are the most authentic, real people you will ever meet. You never have to guess if a baby is being honest with you because they have no choice but to be who they are.

I have always enjoyed observing babies with their moms in the checkout lines of stores. If the little one sees someone they like, their entire face lights up with a smile and maybe a giggle. If they see someone they don't like, they can burst out in tears in a flash.

There is no filter on their emotions. When they are hurt, they cry. When they are happy, they squeal with delight. When they are content, they rest. Adults, on the other hand, are far more complex in the way they express themselves. We smile when we are angry. We are stoic when we are hurting, and we appear friendly at times when we really feel bitter.

I can remember being with my dad when I was all grown up and had children of my own. Sometimes he would say something to me that was hurtful, and in that moment, I felt like a five year old again that wanted to cry. Of course I never did, but the child inside of me was touched by the familiar anger I experienced when I was little.

But since *big boys don't cry*, I sucked up my emotions and buried them deep inside. In the adult world we live in, it is not safe to wear your heart on your sleeve. We are afraid that people will judge us and reject us if they knew how we really feel, so we keep the charade going.

I do want to say that there is a measure of wisdom we need to steward in the way we handle our emotions. Transparency is not meant as a license to recklessly blast people with unchecked emotions. However, many dear folks have been so disconnected from their hearts that a false veneer has formed around them that prevents them from being truly real.

My prayer is that God would give us all the ability to get in touch with our own hearts and all that goes with it. Whether it is the things that make us come alive or the things that make us want to cry. The more we can return to a place of childlike authenticity, the more we will be able to be honest with ourselves and others.

As far as Papa is concerned, He sees beyond your veneer and He loves the little child that you are in His sight. Even when you pretend to be something different, God continues to love the real you and He wants *you* to love and respect the real you as well.

I have heard it said that the anointing God has for a person can only flow through them when they are being who God intended them to be in the first place. Living your life should be the easiest, most natural thing you can do because that is how God designed you to live.

However, if you feel you are not loveable the way you are, you will spend your life trying to be someone else. If you feel like you need to transform yourself into someone else's expectation of what you should be, you will never be comfortable in your own skin and will live a tireless life of people pleasing.

If you live a life comparing yourself to others and it results in you feeling inadequate and disqualified, then perhaps it is time to rethink the way you see yourself. Think about this for a moment: God has never made the same thing twice. Every snowflake is an original. Every blade of grass a work of art. And every strand of DNA is a one-of-a-kind masterpiece. When your Heavenly Father created you, He threw out the mold!

When we really believe that Almighty God loves us completely, we will experience a new freedom to just be ourselves. It is in this authentic place that people will get to see the reflection of the true image of God that He always intended for us to be.

I believe the safety and security that love brings will position our hearts to be reconnected with our heads and the world around us. No longer will we need to live under the lie that people would reject us if they really knew us.

Little kids have no problem with this concept. They are simply themselves until the adult world around them teaches them otherwise. May God give you the grace to return to your God designed origins, so you can emote the emotions He has entrusted you with.

Ephesians 2:10
For we are God's masterpiece. He has created us anew in Christ Jesus, so we can do the good things he planned for us long ago. (NLT)

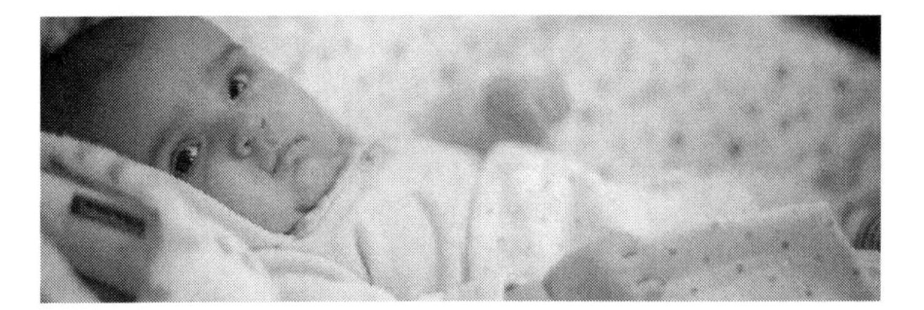

-32-
LITTLE CHILDREN ARE DEFENSELESS

Tiny babies can barely hold up their own head, let alone protect themselves. They are completely vulnerable and defenseless. There is absolutely nothing they can do to ensure their safety. So how do they manage life in such a weakened state? The obvious answer is they have full, unrestricted access to all of the strength and resources that come from their parents.

Since Almighty God is our true Father, it only stands to reason that as His beloved children, we have the same full, unrestricted access to all of His strength and resources too. Or do we? The simple answer is a resounding *yes*, but unfortunately it does not appear to be that simple for those of us who see the world through an adult mindset.

The broken systems of the kingdoms of this world teach us that if we don't fight for ourselves, nobody else will. If we don't build up walls of self-protection around us, we can get hurt. If we don't spend our lives in the pursuit of things that will keep us safe, we will not be secure.

We live in a *dog eat dog* world where we are burned out,

stressed out, maxed out, exhausted, frustrated, fearful, and disillusioned. We have to fight for what we get and we have to fight to keep it. Even in church life, we are not insulated from such broken mindsets. We are often taught that God's love for us is conditional on our performance and that even our salvation can be lost if we misstep.

In some religious circles, God is portrayed as a schizophrenic deity that loves us one minute and is ready to smite us the next. Though the word *grace* does get mentioned, it is only used at convenient times and only serves to add more confusion to what they define as the love of God.

So if the world systems can't keep us safe and many of the church systems can't either, what is a person to do? The simple answer is to return to the place of complete safety and security that a little child enjoys. After all, you've got the biggest, best Dad in the universe!

God is Father and fathers protect their kids. I am a father and a grandfather, so I know a little something about this. If a person slapped me across the face, I would hope to have the grace to turn the other cheek. However, if someone tried to hurt my children or grandchildren, all bets are off. They would see a side of me that they would wished they had never seen.

God has always had a protective heart towards those He loves. In most cases, Israel was outnumbered and outgunned and yet the promise of God was that He would fight for them. Exodus 14:14 says, "The Lord himself will fight for you. Just stay calm" (NLT).

If you want a picture of a protected life living in the shadow of the Almighty, read Psalm 91. We read of a secret place, a fortress, surrounded by angels that are committed to the care of little ones. We read of wings of protection, shields and deliverance from enemies. This is the place where God wants us to live every day of our lives.

We can get another glimpse of our Father's protective heart, especially for little children, in Matthew 18:5-6 when Jesus tells His disciples the devastating consequences of those who want to harm His little ones:

5 Whoever receives one such little child in my name receives me, 6 but whoever causes one of these little ones who believe in me to stumble, it would be better for him that a huge millstone should be hung around his neck, and that he should be sunk in the depths of the sea (WEB).

Yikes!

The intended order of things is that little kids were meant to live under the watchful eye of their loving parents. And as a result, the safety and security they experience would free them from being preoccupied by things that could harm them.

May God give you the grace to return to the place of feeling protected, so you can boldly declare to those around you, "If God is for us, who can ever be against us?" (Romans 8:31 NLT)

I pray you would become oblivious to the surrounding perils of this world and know that you don't have to live your life in self-protection any longer because your Dad's got your back.

Psalm 116:6
The Lord protects those of childlike faith; I was facing death, and he saved me (NLT).

-33- LITTLE CHILDREN ARE FEARLESS

Our granddaughter Riley is fearless. She will boldly go places oblivious to the dangers around her. Of course, as she gets older, she will learn to respect things that could cause her harm. A hot stove can burn her, fast moving cars on the street are dangerous, etc.

The reason little children are fearless is because they haven't had the negative life experiences yet that cause them to be afraid. If they haven't reached out and touched a burning candle on a birthday cake, they won't be afraid of the flame. As they grow, they learn to fear more things.

Fear in itself isn't a bad thing. It is a necessary part of our lives that helps us to respect things that could hurt us, so we can then be wise and keep our distance from anything harmful. For example, a healthy fear of sharks will keep me from swimming in a shark tank.

There was a time years ago when I was camping that I ended up being chased by a bear. For that moment, fear of being killed by the bear energized me to outrun it; fear was my biggest motivator. However, if I had nightmares about that experience and was terrorized long after the incident was over, I would have transitioned into a very unhealthy place of living in fear. It is what we do with fear that makes all the difference in the world.

If we try and negotiate with fear and allow it to co-exist in our lives, we will live life boxing with shadows. Worse yet, if we agree with the fearful thoughts that enter our head, we will give power to an enemy that is only too happy to expand its influence in our lives.

Think of it this way: If a fearful thought knocks at the front door of my house and I invite it in, I may think it is only welcome in the front foyer. The thing with fear is that it will not be happy just to have a tiny place in your home; it will continue to try to expand its influence until it occupies every room in my house.

We know that God has not given us a spirit of fear (2 Timothy 1:7). So where does unhealthy fear originate? Fear is rooted in a foundational lie that tries to convince us that we are fatherless, helpless and all alone. Fear sows seeds of unbelief into every circumstance, hoping we will choose to believe it rather than God.

Fear finds its origins in the basic premise that God does not really love us, so we have to proactively protect ourselves by entertaining anxious, fearful thoughts in order to avert every impending disaster. Jesus exposed the root of fear when He described the devil as the father of lies (John 8:44). He goes on to say that when the enemy lies to us, he is speaking his native language.

There is absolutely no truth in him. He is a master legalist though, and he knows the Bible better than we do, so he is skilled at twisting and perverting God's good intent with hopes that we might believe his deception.

Our Big Brother Jesus came to destroy the works of the devil (1 John 3:8) and to free us from the fear of death that has enslaved us all our lives (Hebrews 2:14-15). He came to save us, redeem us, and reconcile us (2 Corinthians 5:18-20) back to the One who is the very expression of love itself.

When we live in love, God lives in us and we live in Him (1 John 4:16). In this secure place of abiding in our Father's goodness, fear has no choice but to flee. Love does not negotiate with fear. Love violently expels fear in the same way that Jesus cast out devils.

There was a time in my life where I felt vulnerable because of the exposure we had, having a worldwide influence on the Internet. I don't know when it happened, but at some point, I must have agreed with the lying, fearful thoughts that were knocking at my door. The result was a terrifying battle with fear that lasted for many months.

At times, these fearful thoughts would cause me to hyperventilate and break out into sweats. Of course, I would rebuke the lies and quote Scripture, but the relief I experienced during those times was only temporary.

It was during this very difficult season in my life that I felt led to create a new website called 365promises.com. Even though I was battling fear personally, I was hanging on to God's promises for dear life as I developed this new web strategy.

Then one day, the fear was dealt a deathblow in my life. It wasn't as a result of my own great faith or spiritual disciplines. I really didn't do anything different than I had done so many times before in order to kick fear out of my house.

I was just sitting on the couch in our living room recounting to my wife my ongoing struggle with fear. It was as if Ann was looking through me when she said the words, "Leave that little boy alone!" With great authority, she slapped me on the chest and at that moment, I had a picture in my spirit.

The scene was set on a school playground and I was a little two-year-old boy, cowering in the presence of fear. A three hundred pound biker dude, who was yelling at me and doing his best to intimidate me, portrayed the spirit of fear. Then it happened: In this vision, my Heavenly Father came on to the playground.

Up until that time, I had experienced many different expressions of God's love that would calm, comfort and strengthen me. But for the first time in my life, I experienced the ferocious, protective, parental love that God had for me.

It was funny because when this tattoo laden expression of fear got one glimpse of my Heavenly Dad coming onto the playground, it was so terrified that it self imploded and was no more. That was the day I experienced the perfect love that casts out fear (1 John 4:18).

I have always appreciated Zephaniah 3:17. "For the Lord your God is living among you. He is a mighty savior. He will take delight in you with gladness. With his love, he will calm all your fears. He will rejoice over you with joyful songs" (NLT).

I have usually focused on the part of the verse where God delights and sings over us, but now, after experiencing a love that is 'mighty to save', I see the ferocious Fatherheart of God in a brand new way.

There are many passages in the Bible where God says, "Do not fear." He wouldn't tell us that unless there was something to be afraid of. The reality is, there are many things that happen in life that will cause our hearts to be afraid. It isn't the fear that is the issue, but what we do with it.

The day fear was vanquished in the presence of my loving Father was a day I will never forget. Nothing in my circumstances changed that day. The only thing that *did* change was my response to the lying, fearful thoughts that the enemy was trying to sow in my mind.

I believe that this encounter with ferocious fatherly affection prepared me and my wife for the day when fear would raise its ugly head again, on a level far greater than anything we have ever experienced before. And that was when our daughter was diagnosed with a very aggressive form of Leukemia.

I'm not saying we weren't afraid, because we were. I think it would be more accurate to say we were terrified at the prospects that were facing our daughter. I think a life threatening illness is every parent's worse nightmare, so it is understandable that we would be afraid. But in the midst of the deepest darkness we have ever encountered in our lives, we heard the voice of our Father saying:

Isaiah 41:10
Don't you be afraid, for I am with you. Don't be dismayed, for I am your God. I will strengthen you. Yes, I will help you. Yes, I will uphold you with the right hand of my righteousness (WEB).

At the time of this writing, we are past the midway point of our daughter's twenty-eight months of near daily chemotherapy treatment. There are good days and there are bad days. There are days when things cause us to be afraid. But it is at these times, we run into Papa's arms to find comfort that drives fear out of our little hearts.

There is no question that we will have trouble on this side of heaven because of the consequences of a broken, fallen world. Some of these troubles will cause us to be afraid. God understands that little kids get scared. He just wants us to bring every fear we have to Him so He can deal with it.

My prayer is that the perfect love of God would drive every ounce of fear out of your life. May you experience the ferocious, protective parental love of God in every circumstance you face. May you be awakened to see love at work in the midst of every situation.

The Apostle Paul said he was *persuaded* that nothing could ever separate him from the love of God in Christ (Romans 8:35-39). When I read that Paul was persuaded, I think he was saying that there was a time when he didn't know that to be the truth. That is why he needed to be persuaded in the first place.

May the ferocious love of your Papa convince you, persuade you, and draw you into a place of safety and security in the midst of every storm you and your loved ones are facing. May His ferocious love eclipse any effort of the enemy that tries to separate you from the peace of knowing you are safe in His arms. After all, from God's perspective, you are a much loved little child under His care.

Romans 8:37
No, in all these things, we are more than conquerors through him who loved us (WEB).

-34- LITTLE CHILDREN ARE FREE

God is all about freedom. He is completely free and it is His heart that we would be free too. Jesus told us in John 8:36 that whom the Son sets free, is free indeed. Galatians 5:1 tells us it is for freedom's sake Christ has set us free.

So there is absolutely no question that freedom is a big part of God's plan and His purpose for our lives. As a matter of fact, it is impossible to be imprisoned in God's presence because 2 Corinthians 3:17 says, "Now the Lord is the Spirit, and where the Spirit of the Lord is, there is freedom (NIV)".

Little kids are a beautiful example of freedom that we should take note of. They are free from people pleasing and they are free from overthinking things. They are who they are and they live each day in this glorious simplicity.

Of course there are boundaries to their freedom, but these safeguards are meant to protect them, not hurt them. Mom and dad lock the doors so their little ones can't go outside into the street. But within the walls of their house, they are free to run and play and imagine.

As we grow up, we lose our ability to enjoy a free life. Employers put all kinds of demands on us. People place all kinds of unrealistic expectations on us. Culture bombards us with thousands of media messages a day telling us who we should be and what we should buy. And maybe, just maybe, even church life might add a few links to the chains that bind us.

I think it is safe to say that as we grow, we don't learn to be free, we un-learn it. The more we are aware of the world around us, the more we lose our own personal sense of freedom. We use words like *responsibility* or being *practical* in our effort to justify our inability to live free.

But what if it has always been God's heart for you to be free from all of the trappings in society? What if He actually is happy when He sees His kids walking in real freedom? Often, people who are free can irritate us. They may be called 'non-conformists' or 'rebellious' because they aren't towing the company line.

But what if there is a freedom of heart God wants us to enjoy that does indeed free us from the hamster wheel of performance and compliance? I'm not saying we should rebel for the sake of rebellion. The Apostle Paul is clear in Galatians 5:13 that we are not to abuse the freedom given to us to indulge in sinful desires, but *rather, serve one another humbly in love.* I'm not talking about that kind of freedom. I'm talking about the freedom to be you…unrestrained.

A few years back, I went to a local zoo to take some photos of big game animals I thought might inspire me. It was a very hot mid summer afternoon, so it probably wasn't an appropriate time to see the animals at their best. Most of them were asleep in an attempt to manage the sweltering heat. Naturally, I felt disappointed.

To be honest, when I entered the zoo I had this overwhelming sense that I had just walked into a prison. Instead of being inspired, I felt oppressed and discouraged. Since God was speaking to me a lot about lions in those days, I thought I would check out the lion exhibit.

When I walked up to the lion cage, both the male and the female were sound asleep. I took a photo of them sleeping and prayed a simple prayer to Papa. I told Him I would really like it if the male lion would open his eyes so I could take a photo.

At that very moment, the lion opened his eyes and it felt like he was staring right through me. I snapped the photo and I heard the Lord say, "Take a look at this lion. This is why I hate captivity." I knew God wasn't speaking about the moral issues surrounding zoos; He was speaking about the condition of the human heart.

Since God created a lion to naturally be the king of the jungle, seeing him imprisoned in a very small cage was the most unnatural of sights to behold. The imagery continued as I was reminded that the Lion of Judah (Revelation 5:5) dwelt in the hearts of every believer around the world.

When I looked into the eyes of this lion, I could see that he knew who he was, but there was nothing he could do to take back his freedom. Unlike this lion, we are truly free because of what Jesus did but many of us don't know it. As a result, we live our lives in prison cells that have no doors to hold us captive. But, we choose to stay there anyway.

A few months later, I had the opportunity to go to another zoo and I had yet another lion encounter. Once again, the male lion was sound asleep so I asked Papa to wake him up. It wasn't long before he woke up. He made his way to a part of the exhibit where there were people three rows deep, all trying to take pictures.

I was at the back of the crowd and felt like Zacchaeus when he climbed a tree to sneak a peak at Jesus (Luke 19:1-10). I climbed onto a rock that was above the crowd so I could have an eye-to-eye level view with the lion. He seemed to be a little agitated.

It felt like he was looking at me square in my eyes as he let out a roar that penetrated the very fabric of my being. I felt a strong sense of God's presence come over me while the lion roared and I heard God say, "I did this for you because I wanted you to experience the roar of a lion."

I have heard it said that when a lion roars in the jungle, it can be heard for miles away. I believe that in the same way a lion roars to its enemies to declare its territory, Papa wants us to roar the declaration of freedom in our lives.

Since my encounters with the lions, I have led people in many different places and continents in corporate roars of freedom. I have always encouraged them to declare their freedom in their mother tongue, to signify they are free from the things in their own culture that may try to enslave them.

May God give you the boldness of a lion (Proverbs 28:1) and the faith to return to a place where you can live truly free; free from cultural demands and free from the expectations of people.

And may the Spirit of the Sovereign Lord truly set you free (Isaiah 61:1) so you can return to the untethered heart of a child who is just who God made them to be. After all, all creation is groaning and waiting to be brought into the freedom and the glory of God's own kids.

Romans 8:19-21
19 For the creation waits in eager expectation for the children of God to be revealed. 20 For the creation was subjected to frustration, not by its own choice, but by the will of the one who subjected it, in hope 21 that the creation itself will be liberated from its bondage to decay and brought into the freedom and glory of the children of God (NIV).

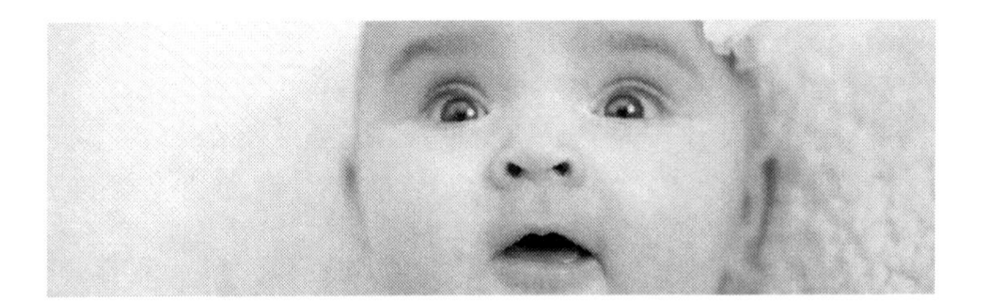

-35-
LITTLE CHILDREN HAVE GREAT FAITH

If spiritual maturity is measured by how much we are able to trust God and believe all that He says is true, those among us with a childlike heart would be considered the greatest. At least, that is what Jesus thinks (Matthew 18:1-5).

If you have ever questioned why Jesus said the greatest in God's Kingdom are little kids, look no further than their amazing ability to believe and to trust. There is not a greater example of faith in this world today than the faith of a little kid.

If a parent tells a little child that the sky is purple, then the little one believes it. If mom or dad says that elephants can fly, then the open, trusting heart of a child shouts yay! There is no doubt, no suspicion, no unbelief, and no cynicism in their hearts. They simply believe everything they are told.

If we try and see the Kingdom of God through an adult mindset, we will miss the whole point of what the Christian life is all about. If God is indeed the head of His family (Ephesians 3:14-15), there would be a basic assumption that whatever Father says is true. If He says we can heal the sick, it's true. If He says we can raise the dead, it's true. No questions.

No suspicion. No doubts whatsoever.

I believe one of the reasons that we struggle to believe what God says is true is because we don't relate to our Father as a little child. We think He expects us to be competent, strong, independent and worthy of His trust. When in fact, it is the absolute opposite of these attributes that He considers really amazing.

But the truth is, God created you with a really great ability to believe and trust. From the moment you were born, your open heart was ready to believe everything your parents said to you because that is how God intended it to be. You were designed with great faith.

The problem was never with *you*. The problem was with the broken orphan hearted world system in which you entered. If the childlike awe and wonder you had as a little kid was nurtured and encouraged, you would have no problem believing today. Unfortunately as we grow up, one by one, all of the things that made life magical as a little child are taken away from us.

When I was a little boy, I really thought there was a jolly fat man in a red suit who came to our house once a year. I can remember thinking that I heard the hoof sounds of reindeer on our roof and I would squeal with delight. When I would lose a tooth, there was no doubt a fairy would come in the middle night and replace the tooth with a quarter under my pillow.

I believed my dad was the strongest dad in the entire world. I believed in rocket ships, far away lands, dinosaurs and many, many other magical things. Then one by one, I awakened to the harsh reality that what I thought was true, was in fact untrue. Trust, belief and wonder were replaced with doubt, suspicion and cynicism.

No wonder adults have a hard time believing in God. We have had our childlike faith kicked right out of us. How are we supposed to now believe that there are angels surrounding us wherever we go? How are we supposed to believe that God Himself has made His dwelling place in our hearts? How are we supposed to believe that there is an eternal Kingdom awaiting us filled with unimaginable treasures?

The only way we can ever hope to believe in the unbelievable again is to return to the place in our hearts where we first lost our ability to believe and trust. And that is when we were very, very little.

My prayer is that we would all see the high value that our Father has placed on us believing Him just like a child does. The thing is, it takes great risk to expose ourselves again to a magical world of angels and rainbows and Kingdoms.

However, if we are ever going to speak to mountains and watch them be thrown into the sea, it will only be when we return to a childlike view of the world again (Mark 11:23).

1 Corinthians 13:7 says, "love believes all things." Little children believe all things until what they believe is stolen from them. Papa God wants to restore your ability to believe the unbelievable. He wants to heal every wound in your heart where innocence was stolen so you can live a life filled with wonder again.

Would you be willing to abandon your adult sized cynicism and exchange it for the immeasurable amount of faith and trust your Father first wove into your DNA in your mother's womb? My prayer is that you would respond just like a little child would and simply say YAY!

-36-
LITTLE CHILDREN NEED SIMPLICITY

If you sat down with a five year old and tried to explain Einstein's theory of relativity, what kind of response would you get? Probably a blank stare. If you tried to explain the law of thermodynamics, the little child would probably just get bored and walk away.

However, if you got on the floor with this little one and had an imaginary tea party, you would capture their attention for hours upon end. If our ability to reason is primarily in the left brain and our ability to imagine and create is in the right brain, I'm thinking little kids are mostly right brainers.

And as such, they need everything to be simplified for them. They simply cannot comprehend complexities beyond their pay grade. I kind of think that is one of the things Jesus especially likes about little kids; they are simple through and through.

Before Jesus came on the scene two thousand years ago, the broken religious system had so complicated a relationship with God that it was impossible to fulfill every requirement. The religious leaders would tell the people what they could and couldn't do. Only on *certain* days and in *certain* ways were *certain* things even allowed. However, if you did the right thing on the wrong day, you were in trouble.

On and on they added more and more rules, laws and conditions that were intended to qualify a person to have a relationship with God and it all became really unmanageable. Then Jesus came along and simply and basically said, if you love God and love others as yourself, you don't need to do anything else (Matthew 22:36-40).

The Pharisees made a simple relationship with God very complicated. Jesus made the unfathomable love of God amazingly simple. The Pharisees couldn't even call Yahweh by His name and Jesus taught His disciples to call God… "Father" (Matthew 6:9-13).

I am convinced that if we share a gospel message that is too complicated for little children to grasp, it is simply too complicated, period. In many religious circles, we have embraced Old Testament law based principles and added a little bit of New Testament ideology and called it Christianity.

We have communicated to the masses that in order for us to be accepted by God, we have to give enough, read enough, serve enough and jump through all of the right hoops, or else.

Early in my Christian life I was told, "Those who love the church attend Sunday mornings. Those who love the pastor attend Sunday night and those who love God come out to Wednesday night services!" Wow! Is that demanding or what?

I am so glad I learned that this form of Christianity is not Christianity at all. It may bring about an appearance of godliness but it exists without the substance of relationship. I would be psychotic to tell my kids they are no longer my children if they don't fulfill a bunch of do's and don'ts. But unfortunately many people within the church and outside of the church think that is what being a Christian is all about.

The life God has called us to live is to simply enjoy the unchangeable, unwavering fact that we are His kids (1 John 3:1). And because we are His kids, we have free access to His throne room, day or night (Hebrews 4:16).

The truth of the gospel is simply this: Jesus died so that His Father could become our Father (John 20:17). And as the Father of our spirit (Hebrews 12:9), He promises to be a real Dad to us in every way possible (2 Corinthians 6:18). He is the One who protects us, provides for us, encourages us, comforts us, teaches us, strengthens us, and loves us every minute of every day this side of heaven.

My prayer is that God would give you the grace to return to the simplicity of a little child who knows completely and fully that you are loved and cared for. May the complexities of a broken religious system that have been drummed into you be replaced by a childlike heart, whose only prayer is to cry out 'Abba, Father!'

Romans 8:15-17
15 For you didn't receive the spirit of bondage again to fear, but you received the Spirit of adoption, by whom we cry, "Abba! Father!" 16 The Spirit himself testifies with our spirit that we are children of God; 17 and if children, then heirs; heirs of God, and joint heirs with Christ; if indeed we suffer with him, that we may also be glorified with him (WEB).

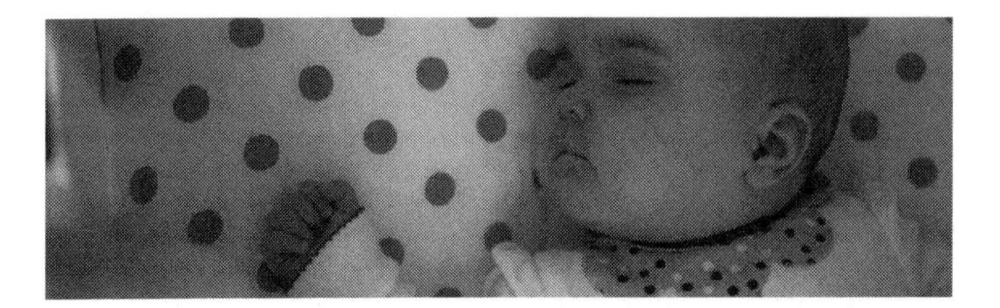

-37- LITTLE CHILDREN KNOW HOW TO REST

Since my granddaughter was born, one of my favorite things to do is to sneak into her room and just watch her as she sleeps. With her arms stretched over her head, she is the perfect picture of peace and rest.

As she has gotten a bit older, she has now learned how to sleep in some of the most unusual of positions. I laughed out loud the other day when my daughter, Kristin, showed me a photo of Riley sound asleep in a seated position with her face buried in her little feet. I can remember seeing photos of myself sound asleep with my face planted on the sidewalk when I was just a little older than Riley. So, I can say she gets it honestly.

Little children can go one hundred miles per hour one minute and then conk out and slip off into a deep sleep the next. They know how to step on the accelerator and they know when to step on the brakes. Their life is a beautiful balance of high energy and deep rest.

While little ones have no problem resting when they are tired, many adults struggle to find the deep rest that seems so natural to children. If you have ever wondered why that is the case, let me share some of my thoughts on the subject.

Adults tend to equate their personal value with their productivity. As long as they are producing, they feel a sense of worth. However, when they stop working or achieving, their value equation changes. I think that is why retirement can be so devastating for some people. Everything that has defined them for their entire career has suddenly ceased to exist. Apart from the value work brings, who are they?

I think this fear of becoming disconnected from what society has perceived as valuable is one of the motivating factors that makes it hard to rest in our adult world. If there were just three questions you could ask a person when you first meet them, they might be: 1) What is your name? 2.)Where do you live? 3) What do you do?

It is the 'What do you do?' question that is so connected with our wellbeing that often we find it impossible to truly find meaning apart from our doing. And yet we are called human *beings*, not human *doings*. As a high achieving, type A personality who spent his entire life in search of an elusive affirmation that came through hard work, I found it difficult to rest. Even when I came into the revelation of Papa's love for me, I still had a pretty strong drive to succeed.

I can remember being at a South African leaders' meeting with Jack Winter once, and he told the group, "God doesn't want you to slow down, He wants to remove your engine." Think about that statement for a minute. The rest that God wants us to enter into is not one where we simply decelerate a little bit. The rest that He intends us to embrace will result in us surrendering every ounce of our human effort to Him as a sweet smelling sacrifice.

Quite a few years ago, I had a practical encounter with the kind of rest that Abba desires for us, when my wife and I embarked on a short retreat to seek God's direction for the next season. We both had sensed that there was a time of transition coming for our ministry, so we wanted to take time away to hear His heart for us.

I came fully prepared with all of my study Bibles and resources to dig deep into God's Word to discover what His next step for us was. The first thing I did was turn on a very old archaic electronic Bible I hadn't used for years. The last verse I'd read on this device popped up on the screen when it booted up.

It was a very short verse from Psalm 46:10, "Be still and know that I am God." The crazy thing is I couldn't get past this one little verse for the next four days! The Hebrew word for 'be still' is '*raw-faw*' which Strong's Concordance defines as '*to cease, slacken, forsake, leave, let alone and be slothful*'.

There was absolutely no question what Papa was saying to me. He said, "Barry, I want you to stop *everything*." When God said to stop everything, He meant everything. The month before, I had completely redesigned the Father's Love Letter website to run automatically without my daily assistance, so that part was easy to do.

But part of the deal to stop everything was also to stop directly selling Father's Love Letter resources, which was our main source of income. When I asked God how we would get by, He responded by saying, "Let Me take care of you." So we stopped selling resources and I stopped traveling internationally.

I honestly thought this short sabbatical might last a month or two, and then something else would open up. But it didn't. In the third month of my inactivity, I heard the Lord say to me, "Consider yourself retired until further notice." While that sounds all nice and well, at forty-eight years of age, I didn't have a retirement income so I didn't know what to do!

Yet, God continued to provide for us every month in unexpected ways. I can remember at one point, we were invited to stay with friends in one of the retirement capitals of the USA: Sarasota, Florida. While sitting on a park bench in the city center with a bunch of 'blue hairs' and old gaffers, I was once again reminded that the Lord had retired me from active service.

The only thing I kept doing in this season was teaching at local Bible schools and conferences. When I would attend some of these events, I would inevitably bump into ministry friends who would ask me where I was traveling and what was new in our ministry.

The funny thing was, Papa was very specific in the way He wanted me to answer their questions about my activity. He told me, "Barry, when people ask you what you are doing, I want you to look right into their eyes, give them a big smile and tell them you are doing NOTHING and don't explain why."

This was one of the hardest things I had to do in this season. All of a sudden, conversations turned a tad awkward as people didn't know how to respond after I told them I wasn't doing a thing. Of course, everything inside of me wanted to explain myself so they wouldn't think I must have had a mental breakdown, but Papa said no.

Months turned into a year and then into eighteen months of doing nothing. The pressure to do *something* was almost unbearable. I can remember the day when I was so frustrated by my lack of productivity, I cried out to God and said, "If I don't do something, what right do I have to even take one breath?"

Papa brought me right back to the moment ten years earlier when Jack Winter put his arms around me and I had my homecoming. During that special ministry time, Papa had said to me, "Barry, I don't love you because you do anything to deserve it, I love you because you breathe."

After eighteen months of reluctant rest from ministry activity, I was re-centered in my Father's embrace again. At that moment, I realized just how deep my own personal value was still connected to my productivity, and yet all of my achievements had nothing to do with how my Abba loved me.

In Hebrews 4:9-11, we read about an invitation to rest:
9 There remains therefore a Sabbath rest for the people of God. 10 For he who has entered into his rest has himself also rested from his works, as God did from his. 11 Let us therefore give diligence to enter into that rest, lest anyone fall after the same example of disobedience (WEB).

The NIV says we are to "make every effort to enter that rest." The KJV says we are to "labor" to enter God's rest. It seems like a paradox that we have to work to enter into rest but I have learned this in indeed the case. If our broken value system is based on our productivity, it takes great faith to be able to "cease from our own works" and disconnect from all of our dysfunctional ideas of what we think pleases God.

While I was eventually released to travel internationally again, I really have never left that Sabbath rest I was called into back in 2008. I will, from time to time, be drawn back into the wacky world of comparisons where I try to justify myself in the eyes of others. But it is only when I return to the rest of knowing I am loved completely, whether I am preaching to thousands or having a nap, that I can really be still and know by experience that God really is my God.

Many of us are familiar with the invitation that Jesus extends to us to enter His rest in Matthew 11:28-30. In order for us to really enjoy the light burden and easy yoke our Big Brother offers us, we need to read the verses preceding His invitation.

Matthew 11:25-27
25 At that time, Jesus answered, "I thank you, Father, Lord of heaven and earth, that you hid these things from the wise and understanding, and revealed them to infants. 26 Yes, Father, for so it was well-pleasing in your sight. 27 All things have been delivered to me by my Father. No one knows the Son, except the Father; neither does anyone know the Father, except the Son, and he to whom the Son desires to reveal him (WEB).

The revelation of Kingdom rest is reserved for little kids who know their Father loves them. Little children naturally know how to rest because their value is not yet connected to their productivity. They don't strive or earn a living to justify their existence. They just are who they are.

May God give us the grace to return to the simplicity and the peace of a little child who knows they are absolutely, unconditionally loved at work, at play and when they are in the deepest of sleeps.

Matthew 11:28-30
28 "Come to me, all you who labor and are heavily burdened, and I will give you rest. 29 Take my yoke upon you, and learn from me, for I am gentle and humble in heart; and you will find rest for your souls. 30 For my yoke is easy, and my burden is light" (WEB).

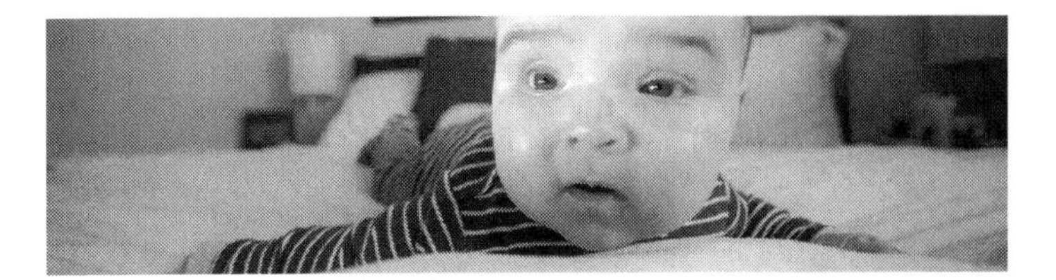

-38-
LITTLE CHILDREN ARE CARE FREE

When our youngest daughter was a little girl, she loved to buy things. She would continually ask me, "Dad, can I have a new toy? Dad, can I have a new dress? Dad, can I have? Can I have? Can I have?" You get the picture.

Often the things she would ask for were more than what we could afford at the time, so I would tell her, "Honey, we don't have the money to get that." As far as Candice was concerned, the solution was simple. Every time I would say we didn't have the money, she would respond by saying, "Just go to the bank, Dad, they've got lots of money!"

From the vantage point of a little girl, money was never an issue; in Candice's eyes, we had an unlimited supply of cash at our disposal. Now of course, the older she got, the more she could grasp the complexities of a financial system where her dad would actually have to pay back any money the bank gave him. But as a little child, she saw no such limitations.

In Matthew 6:25, Jesus says that we are to "take no thought for your life" (KJV) or as other translations say, "Don't be anxious or worried about your life." Have you ever wondered if it is even possible to *take no thought* for your life? I believe it is possible or Jesus wouldn't have said it.

If you look at little kids, you will see a beautiful picture of this in action. The younger they are, the less they have the capacity to worry. They live their lives every day oblivious to the stresses and concerns of the world around them. It is only when they grow up that the weight of the world is placed on their shoulders one brick at a time.

After Jesus tells His disciples to not even think about their daily needs, He tells them why. Because they have a Heavenly Father who loves them so much that He is looking after all the details. Verse 26 says: See the birds of the sky, that they don't sow, neither do they reap, nor gather into barns. Your heavenly Father feeds them. Aren't you of much more value than they (WEB)?

The reason adults worry so much is because they are not yet convinced of their value to God. Little children live under the basic assumption that their parents will look after their every need. This foundational carefree attitude allows them to just be little kids.

It takes a lot of emotional energy to manage worry. Can you imagine how crazy it would be if little kids spent their time worrying about things like adults do? Instead of having fun and frolicking like they are supposed to, they would transform into a very unnatural form of themselves where life would become burdensome.

Any loving parent in the world would quickly stop their child from worrying about paying the mortgage. Why? Because if they spend their time wrapped up in a ball of anxiety over things they can't control, they will be robbed from the joy of living life to its fullest.

I think our Heavenly Father feels the same way about us. As far as He is concerned, worry is a distraction that will steal our fruitfulness (Matthew 13:22). In the same way parents don't want their little ones to be anxious, God wants us to be set free from having to carry the weight of the world on our shoulders.

There was a time in our ministry when the vision to see the Father's Love Letter delivered to every person on the planet became a heavy burden I felt compelled to carry. While the influence of the love letter has went global, command central has always been a very small office in the basement of our very small house.

We have never had a huge budget or ministry staff in which to see this vision fulfilled. There was just me, my wife and a friend of ours, Cheryl, who helped us part time. We were all trying to keep up with the global demands of having 100+ language translations of the Father's Love Letter in circulation.

This burden got so heavy on me that when people asked me what my vision was, I didn't want to tell them any longer. Inevitably, when I would share that I wanted to see the Father's Love Letter delivered to every person in the world, they'd ask how that was going to happen?

I would then feel responsible to give them a competent answer. The only problem was I didn't have one, so the burden just got heavier and heavier. One day, God spoke to me and said He never intended the vision I had to become such a burden.

As a matter of fact, He told me that the vision to see the love letter delivered around the world wasn't my vision, it was His. He reminded me of John 5:19-20 and how Jesus said that the work He was doing wasn't His work, but His Dad's.

John 5:19-20
19 Jesus therefore answered them, "Most certainly, I tell you, the Son can do nothing of himself, but what he sees the Father doing. For whatever things he does, these the Son also does likewise. 20 For the Father has affection for the Son, and shows him all things that he himself does. He will show him greater works than these, that you may marvel (WEB).

Papa especially pointed out verse 20 to me. Because of His great affection for me, He was showing me all the things HE was doing. He said, "Barry, you are part of the family business and because you are My son, I am showing you all that I am doing."

I realized I had been trying to manage a vision that was way too big for me to carry. When I discovered it was my Papa's vision and not my own, it freed me to simply tell other people what I saw my Father doing. No longer did I need to take personal responsibility on how He was going to do it.

The first opportunity for me to test out this new found freedom came when I arrived in Finland for the first time. The host pastor met me at the airport, and during our conversation, he asked me what my vision was. Now, with the simplicity of a little child, I told him I believed my Papa wanted to see the love letter delivered to every home in Finland.

He asked me how I planned to do it and I smiled and said, "I don't know!" A few days later he came back to me and told me he was also an executive for a large ministry organization in Europe, and they were planning a door-to-door Christmas mailing to every home in Finland. Then he asked me if I would be okay if they printed a full color two-sided version of the Finnish Father's Love Letter and delivered it in their mailing to 2.2 million homes. And of course, I happily agreed.

The reality is, in my own ability, I could have never been able to raise the resources to print and distribute the Father's Love Letter to every home in Finland. But when I was able to simply return to the place in my heart of being a little boy with a really BIG Dad, nothing was impossible.

Since that experience, we have seen other ministry organizations come alongside us and deliver the Father's Love Letter door to door in many nations around the world. And the best part about it is, I have had nothing to do with making it happen!

In Matthew 6:8, Jesus reminds us that our Father knows what we need before we even ask Him. He is a good Dad who likes to give good gifts to His kids (James 1:17). He doesn't want you to carry the weight of the world on your shoulders because He is more than able to carry every burden for you.

I want to encourage you today to take every worry or concern you have in your backpack and cast it on the big, strong shoulders of your Heavenly Father. He loves you so much and He wants you to be free to be a little kid again.

He really is your Dad and His heart is to father you in a way that will release you from every care and concern you have.

1 Peter 5:7
Give all your worries and cares to God, for he cares about you (NLT)

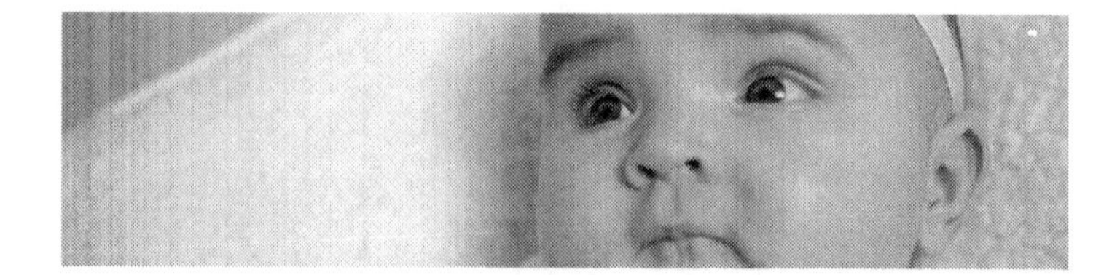

-39-
LITTLE CHILDREN ARE HUMBLE

Little children have the most beautiful humble hearts that you will ever see. They have no developed ego so there is no room for offence to take hold in their heart. They know they are small, weak and helpless and they don't make any apologies for that. They are who they are and they don't spend their lives trying to be something they are not.

That is why Jesus told His disciples in Matthew 18 that true greatness in God's Kingdom is reserved for the childlike. They are simply beautiful empty vessels that naturally display God's glory in a way no adult ever could. When I say *empty vessels*, I mean there is no competing pride that can get in the way of being an unblemished container of God's greatness. C. S. Lewis described humility this way... "True humility is not thinking less of yourself; it is thinking of yourself less."

The root of worry is self-interest. The root of offence is self-importance. The root of many negative emotions is self-protection. Self. Self. Self. There is an entire industry dedicated to propping up 'the great self'. Self-help books fill Christian bookstores. Beauty tips and weight loss strategies are available by the thousands to help make you a better and more beautiful self than ever before.

Little kids are not preoccupied with the great *I*. There is no underlying motive for the way they relate to those around them. Sure, when they are hungry, they let you know. But their lives are not consumed with an unhealthy pursuit of self-importance because they simply don't know what that is. The dictionary.com definition for the word humility is, "*the quality or condition of being humble; modest opinion or estimate of one's own importance, rank, etc.*"

In society, we love to see true humility in our athletes, celebrities and leaders. When the spotlight is shone on a person and they sincerely deflect the attention to include their teammates or those who have helped them, the world takes notice. However, if their ego steps to the main stage and happily boasts about their own personal achievements at the expense of others, the general public will respond with criticism.

Humility in its purest form is a beautiful thing to behold. It has no agenda, it is not easily offended, and is happy to wash the feet of others when needed (John 13:1-5). That is why Jesus said that the greatest among us will be the servant of all (Matthew 23:11).

When we read 1 Corinthians 13:4-8a, it definitely sounds like humility is woven into the very essence of love's substance: 4 Love is patient and is kind; love doesn't envy. Love doesn't brag, is not proud, 5 doesn't behave itself inappropriately, doesn't seek its own way, is not provoked, takes no account of evil; 6 doesn't rejoice in unrighteousness, but rejoices with the truth; 7 bears all things, believes all things, hopes all things, endures all things. 8 Love never fails (WEB).

In some Christian circles, we think of humility as self-hatred, which is diametrically opposed to The Great Commandment (Matthew 22:35-40). Jesus said that we are to love our neighbor as we love ourselves. So if we think biblical humility is hating ourselves, what is the spill over result to our neighbors?

Chances are if you are hard on yourself, you will inevitably be hard on those around you. If you extend grace to yourself, you will be an extender of grace to others. If you love what God loves (and that's YOU!), you will love others in the same way.

Little children who know they are loved have no need to prove anything to anyone. They don't need to be exalted or have their ego stroked. They are secure in who they are and there is no residue of false humility (inverted pride) that can get in the way.

Many years ago, I walked up to a young boy in our church who was an amazing drummer in our worship band. When he started playing with the adult worship team, he was only five years old and was so small that you couldn't see him behind the drum kit. Though he was little in stature, his skill level was really big.

One day after church, I wanted to encourage him, so I said, "Brandon, I think you are awesome." He looked at me with a really big grin on his face and said, "I know!" Now, that's humility at its finest. He was secure in who he was and had no reason to pretend otherwise. He wasn't boasting, but he was comfortable enough to receive my compliment.

If I had said the same words to most adults, they would probably have responded somewhat awkwardly. If King David could say he was "fearfully and wonderfully made" (Psalm 139:14), so can you.

Another example of beautiful childlike humility is when little children pray for adults. There is no adult sized filter on what they pray or how they pray it. They are able to minister in a purity that flows out of the abundance of their hearts in a way adults find extremely difficult.

I once heard a story once of a little boy who was praying for people that were lined up at the church altar when he came to a very large man who was ready to receive prayer. The boy was so small that when he reached up to touch the man's stomach, he could barely get beyond his belt buckle. But when he did touch him, the power of God hit the man so hard that he flew backwards and landed a few feet away on his back.

The boy was so surprised at this man's response to the simple touch of his hand that he stopped for a moment, looked down at his own hand in amazement and said, "Whoa!" When we are truly empty of everything that will try to compete with the fullness of God in us, we can have the freedom to celebrate unapologetically when we see the impossible happen.

2 Corinthians 4:7 says, "But we have this treasure in clay vessels that the exceeding greatness of the power may be of God, and not from ourselves" (WEB). True humility is simply being comfortable with the clay pot that you are, yet at the same time being comfortable with *the exceeding greatness of the power of God* that resides within you.

In one of the few places where Jesus describes Himself, He says, "Take my yoke upon you, and learn from me, for I am gentle and humble in heart; and you will find rest for your souls" (Matthew 11:29 WEB).

Little kids are born with gentle and humble hearts that end up being defiled by the broken world system around them. Jesus told His disciples that they needed to humble themselves and become like little children again if they really wanted to experience all of the wonders of their Father's Kingdom.

Matthew 18:3-5
3 "Most certainly I tell you, unless you turn, and become as little children, you will in no way enter into the Kingdom of Heaven. 4 Whoever therefore humbles himself as this little child, the same is the greatest in the Kingdom of Heaven. 5 Whoever receives one such little child in my name receives me," (WEB).

My prayer is that you would see true humility from God's perspective and embrace it with all your heart. May you see all of the Kingdom's glorious benefits that await those who are willing to repent from their adult ways and return to the beautiful humility of a little child again.

Though God resists the proud, He gives grace to the humble (James 4:6). May you align your heart in such a childlike way that you are positioned under the waterfall of grace, time and time again.

James 4:10
Humble yourselves in the sight of the Lord, and he will exalt you (WEB).

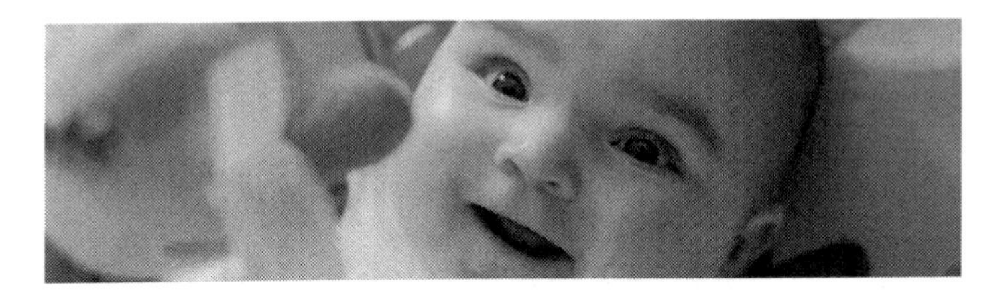

-40-
LITTLE CHILDREN LOVE TO PLAY

Play is a very important part of a little child's day. You might say their day is broken down into four important sections: eating, sleeping, pooping and playing. The older a little child gets, the more they love to play.

Our granddaughter is at a stage right now where she is ready at any moment to launch into play mode whenever there is a willing participant. I love to see the sheer joy she expresses when we are in the full throttle of playtime. Sometimes she is so excited that she clenches both fists, tightens all the muscles in her body and squeals with absolute delight.

While playtime is fun for her, I think it is even more fun for her grandpa. Not only does it help me deepen the bond between us, but it helps me re-enter the wonderful world of being a little child that I once lived in long ago.

In the adult world we live in, we often forget how to play. We see play as a non-essential part of life that we have no choice but to exchange for any number of adult sized burdens and responsibilities. As believers, it is easy to get so caught up in our mission in life that we simply can't justify the things we deem as frivolous and meaningless. Unfortunately, our need to play finds itself in that category.

We see this unusual attitude towards 'fun' expressed in church life too. How is it that we are willing to allow a person to cry in church, but if they laugh, it is unacceptable? Sounds kind of strange, doesn't it? But let me ask you this question: If the Kingdom of God belongs to little kids (Luke 18:15-17) and little kids love to play, what do you think the Kingdom is like?

Here is another question. What do you think God's throne room is like? I think if you asked some people, they would probably say that heaven is a very somber place where Father and Son speak to each other using the King James Bible translation. But is that really what heaven is like? C.S. Lewis said, "Joy is the serious business of heaven"[8] and I couldn't agree with him more. Psalm 16:11 says that in God's presence is fullness of joy.

Think about it this way: Jesus told us in Luke 15:7 that there is more joy in heaven when one sinner repents than over the ninety-nine that do not need to repent. If heaven throws a party every time a person enters the Kingdom, and if there are thousands of people in the world coming to Christ every day, heaven must be one party after another!

If you still can't picture it, just read the three parables Jesus told in Luke 15 in response to the Pharisees criticism of Jesus hanging around sinners. All three stories begin with something being lost (a lost sheep, a lost coin and a lost son) and each one ends with a really big party.

So if you are under the impression that heaven is going to be a stoic place, think again. The Godhead absolutely loves to celebrate because in our Father's house (John 14:1-3) there are lots of party rooms.

While Jesus is seated at the right hand of the Father, He isn't sitting apart from His Dad but is in fact resting His head on His Father's bosom. John 1:18 describes it this way: "No one has seen God at any time. The one and only Son, who is in the bosom of the Father, he has declared him" (WEB).

I love this passage from Proverbs 8 where we read about the absolute joy the Godhead experienced while they were speaking the world into existence:

Proverbs 8:30-32
30 I was the architect at his side. I was his constant delight, rejoicing always in his presence. 31 And how happy I was with the world he created; how I rejoiced with the human family! 32 "And so, my children, listen to me, for all who follow my ways are joyful (NLT).

The Hebrew word for 'rejoicing' in this text is the word *saw-khak* which Strong's Concordance defines as "*to laugh, to play, to make merry, to make sport.*" Heaven is definitely a place where there is lots of room to play.

Malachi 4:2 tells us that when the Sun of Righteousness comes with healing in its wings, the only appropriate response is to leap around just like calves do when they are let out of their stall.

The long and short of it all is that your Heavenly Father wants to restore to you the childlike ability to play. He wants you to revisit the place in your life where playtime was a regular part of your priorities. He wants to free you from any sense of guilt you might experience if you set aside time to have fun.

The older brother in the prodigal son story forgot how to play. He saw himself as a slave to his father who was denied even one goat to celebrate with his friends. Obviously, he was sadly misinformed because the father told him he could have had a party any time he wanted to (Luke 15:25-32).

One of my most favorite times when I teach at schools and speak at conferences is when we have a children's party that helps to reactivate the little child within. The party is usually planned at the end of the last meeting, and comes with all the party fixings you would find at any five year old's party: balloons, noisemakers, party hats, and streamers. The works!

It never ceases to amaze me how so many grown ups can easily turn on the switch of the five year old inside of them once they see the benefits of being little boys and girls with a really BIG Dad.

Once, when I was with my First Nations friends in Northern Quebec, I was a little concerned about how the hundreds of people in the conference would respond to the children's party I had planned. What if they just stared at me when I released the balloons into the meeting? What if they weren't willing to get up and dance to the party music? I was worried I might look really stupid if they didn't think it was a very spiritual thing to do.

To try and get them in a party mood, I prepared a bunch of shouts and cheers to help them get in touch with the little boy or girl within, in case they didn't respond to my balloon launch. I'm glad to say I didn't need even one of my motivators to get them in the mood. As a matter of fact, as soon as we launched the balloons into the crowd and started the party music, I completely lost the whole room.

It was such a joy to see so many people freely return to their childlike origins. Dancing broke out instantly as well as lots of singing, shouting, blowing noise makers, batting balloons around and the like. As I stood there and watched so many dear friends who had suffered so much in their background celebrate before the Lord as little kids, I sensed Papa was smiling over His little ones.

There was one school I taught at where I didn't bring the party supplies because the ceiling in the room was far too low to safely release balloons. I didn't tell anyone I usually planned a children's party, but at the final meal of the school, a children's worker randomly showed up with a full range of party supplies.

Apparently, she heard the Lord direct her to give them to the students so they could play outside. Even though I didn't bring the party supplies, Papa had a back up plan. This was a real affirmation to me of just how important it was to our Heavenly Father that His kids learn to have children's parties.

My prayer is that God would give you the grace to make room for more play in your life. Even if you didn't know how to play as a little child, I pray Papa would teach you.

There was a young man at one of the schools that had a father who had no time to play with him when he was little. I was so thrilled to hear his testimony of how He got a vision of His Heavenly Father down on the floor playing with him while Jesus stood at the door, guarding it to make sure Father and son weren't disturbed.

The Kingdom of God is not about eating or drinking but righteousness, peace and joy in the Holy Spirit (Romans 14:17). Joy is a charter member of the Kingdom and is a very important part of the life of every son and daughter.

Jesus spoke to His disciples about the priority of joy in John 15:11… I have spoken these things to you, that my joy may remain in you, and that your joy may be made full (WEB).

May your joy tank be filled to overflowing today as you learn how to play in your Papa's presence.

Psalms 16:11
You will show me the path of life. In your presence is fullness of joy. In your right hand there are pleasures forever more (WEB).

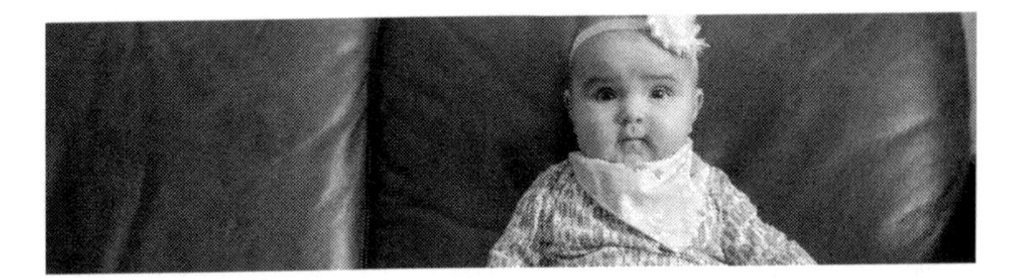

-41-
LITTLE CHILDREN AREN'T AFRAID TO ASK

When our oldest daughter was five or six, she wanted a kitten. The problem was, her dad wasn't even remotely interested in having a kitten. So Kristin did what every little girl would do and went to her grandparents to get their help.

My mom and dad mapped out a strategy with Kristin on how she could wear me down until I would finally say yes to the kitten. I started to find little love notes from my daughter all around the house. "Daddy, I love you! Can I please have a kitten?"

The notes started appearing everywhere. Under my pillow, in my shaving bag, stuffed in my pockets. "Daddy, I love you! Can I please have a kitten? Pretty please!" I am sure you know where this story is going. In no way did I want a cat in our house. I have never been especially fond of them as I have always been a dog person, but because of my little girl's continual, non-stop wearing me down, she got her kitten.

And to be honest, I didn't mind one bit. I was so impressed with her tenacity and her unique ability to pull on my heart strings. I was like putty in her hands. If moms and dads are meant to be an imperfect glimpse of the heart of our Heavenly

Father, how much more is God affected when His kids come to Him?

Jesus speaks of this very subject in Matthew 7:7 when He encourages people to keep on asking. "Ask and keep on asking and it will be given to you; seek and keep on seeking and you will find; knock and keep on knocking and the door will be opened to you"(AMP) .

It is not like we have to wear down our Heavenly Father. However, I do think there is something in the persistence of a little child that touches our Dad's heart.

When our children were little and would ask for something, one of the most dangerous words I could say to them was the word, *maybe*. In the optimistic heart of a little child, the word *maybe* is the crack in the door they need to keep on asking until they get what they want.

I believe our Father loves it when we acknowledge that He is the source of every good and perfect gift (James 1:17). He loves it when we posture our hearts like little kids do with their parents when they ask for what they need.

I was in Kiev, Ukraine quite a few years ago and had the opportunity to pray for one of the leaders at the end of a school. This dear friend shared with me that she had faith to ask God for anything for other people, but when she asked for anything for herself, she felt awkward.

As we continued to discuss this blockage in her heart, I discovered that her earthly father would sometimes make her feel awkward when she asked him for things that were really important to her. So it was quite understandable why she struggled to ask her Heavenly Father for things. It is not rocket science to realize that our experiences with our earthly fathers can negatively influence the way we relate to our Heavenly Father.

By this time, my friend Linda, was in tears because of the memories that surfaced of her childhood. At that moment, I heard God speak to me. He said, "My daughter hasn't asked me for anything. You tell her that she can have anything she wants right now."

The word *anything* kind of rocked my world a bit. What if she asked for something that was impossible? She would be even more disappointed. But of course, it is not wise to try to argue with the Most High. In fear and trembling, I told her what I heard God say.

As soon as I said she could have anything she wanted, she stopped crying, popped her head up in absolute delight and said, "Anything?" My heart sunk right then and there because I knew she was going to ask for something impossible. She then said, "I want my hot water back!"

When we first arrived in Kiev a week earlier, we enjoyed hot water in the apartment we were in. But halfway through the week, the hot water was shut off through a municipal program intended to conserve energy in the warm summer months. And there was no plan for the hot water to be turned back on again any time soon.

Therefore, when my friend asked for hot water, I braced myself for disappointment and went back to my apartment. It wasn't long until I received a phone call from her. All she could say over and over again was, "The hot water is back! The hot water is back!"

Since we lived in the same complex, I thought I would be blessed by this miracle too. But when I checked my taps, I only had cold water. Papa had only turned on the hot water for His little girl simply because she asked for it!

I am so glad that she had faith for me too, because she prayed that I would get my hot water back as well and I did! Over the years, we have kept in touch and Linda always refers to this 'hot water moment' that serves as a marker for her of the goodness of her Heavenly Father.

I want to encourage you to return to the place of childlike persistence in making your requests to God. He loves it when you keep on asking, keep on seeking and keep on knocking. If broken, earthly fathers give good gifts when their children ask them for things, how much more will your *Heavenly Father* give good gifts to those who ask?

May God's love bring healing to every part of your heart where your parents misrepresented the truth of Father's nature to you. May you be strengthened and encouraged to know you have a Dad in heaven who enjoys giving good gifts to His little ones when they simply have the faith to ask for things.

Matthew 10:29-31
29 "Aren't two sparrows sold for an assarion coin? Not one of them falls on the ground apart from your Father's will, 30 but the very hairs of your head are all numbered. 31 Therefore don't be afraid. You are of more value than many sparrows" (WEB).

-42-
LITTE CHILDREN UNDERSTAND THEIR PARENTS KNOW BEST

Just before Jesus teaches His disciples to pray what we now call *The Lord's Prayer*, He makes a very interesting observation about the attentiveness of His Father. He is contrasting the vain repetitions of the heathen when they pray to their gods, to the way we are to ask our Dad for things.

Matthew 6:7-8
7 In praying, don't use vain repetitions, as the Gentiles do; for they think that they will be heard for their much speaking. 8 Therefore don't be like them, for your Father knows what things you need, before you ask him (WEB).

Little children operate under the basic assumption that their parents know best. Sure, they might throw a hissy fit when they don't get what they want, but deep down in their hearts they have to trust that their parents will give them what they need when they need it.

Of course there is a big difference between what we want and what we need. If we are meant to be just a shadow of true parental love, it only stands to reason that our Heavenly Father knows what we need before we even ask for it on a far deeper level than even the best of parents. I am so glad He knows best and we can trust in His timing to answer our prayers.

Because we live in a generation of instant gratification with things such as microwaves and credit cards, we often are unwilling to wait for anything. If we pray to God for something one day and don't see it fulfilled in what we deem an appropriate time frame, we can get discouraged and assume God isn't listening. If we aren't careful, this disappointment can turn into disillusionment.

I want to encourage you to remember the patriarchs of old. Often, there was a huge gap between the promise and the fulfillment of the promise. Abraham had to wait decades to see the birth of his son, Isaac. David had to endure many trials and many years in between him being anointed as king as a boy and its fulfillment. Moses had a forty-year desert experience as a precursor to him being Israel's deliverer.

There are many other examples in the Bible and in life today where there are huge chunks of time between the promise and the fulfillment. It is how we choose to live our lives within those gaps of time that will determine the quality of life we enjoy. Oftentimes we feel like we are waiting years for things and suddenly Papa provides what we need (or have wanted) in the blinking of an eye. Our family just experienced one of these amazing moments ourselves.

When my earthly dad passed away over fifteen years ago, my brother and I made a commitment to care for my mom the rest of her life. Part of that long-term strategy was to try and find a suitable place where she could live with my wife and I. Over the years, we looked on and off but nothing really materialized.

There were many obstacles in the way to this becoming a reality. Things like finances, selling both of our homes, timing, location, etc. At times, we felt a little discouraged, but we would leave it in the Lord's hands again and forget about it. Then recently (fifteen years later), through a divine set of circumstances that are way too involved to describe, we found the perfect home in the perfect neighborhood.

In the space of just a few weeks, we were able to prepare two houses for sale, list them, sell them and purchase this new home that is custom tailored to our unique needs. At the time of this writing, we have just moved into our new home and are still living in the shock of this promise fulfilled. When we discussed all of the things we wanted in a home, this one pretty much met every detail!

I am so thankful that we have a Father who knows what we need and is attentive to not only our needs, but the core desires of our hearts too.

My prayer is that you would find peace in the gap between the promise made and the promise fulfilled. I pray you would be comforted in knowing that your Heavenly Father has your best interests at heart and you can trust in His timing. He knows what you need before you even ask because He is a good Dad that really cares about even the smallest details in your life.

Matthew 6:30-33
30 But if God so clothes the grass of the field, which today exists, and tomorrow is thrown into the oven, won't he much more clothe you, you of little faith? 31 "Therefore don't be anxious, saying, 'What will we eat?', 'What will we drink?' or, 'With what will we be clothed?' 32 For the Gentiles seek after all these things; for your heavenly Father knows that you need all these things. 33 But seek first God's Kingdom, and his righteousness; and all these things will be given to you as well (WEB).

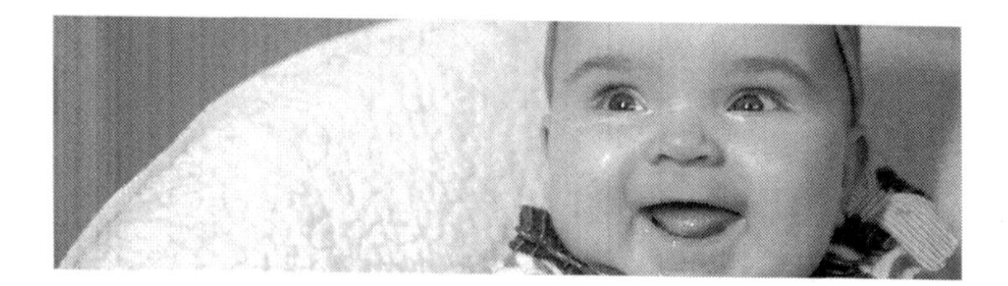

-43-
LITTE CHILDREN LIKE TO SHARE

Our little Riley has now discovered the joy of sharing. At just one year of age, she is now at a place where she loves to give me whatever she has in her hand. Of course, grandpa makes a really big deal out of her generosity, which lights up her little face and makes me smile. To make sure the game goes as intended, I give her back what she gave to me and the cycle continues.

It is beautiful to see something in the hearts of little children where they are happy to share what they have. I can remember watching a news feature on television once where they tested children aged two to six to determine how age factored in their ability to share with others.

It was no surprise that the older the children became, the less willing they were to share. While the two and three year olds were opened handed and happy to mutually exchange whatever they had in their possession, the older children had already learned to hang on with closed fists to everything they had.

Does that sound familiar at all? The bigger we become, the less willing we are to share. In the western world we live in, we drive our own cars, live in our own houses, have our own lawnmowers, etc. without even the faintest desire to share with the community around us. We build fences around our properties, install alarm systems in our cars and homes and barricade our doors. Welcome to the wonderful world of being a grown up.

So what is it exactly in the heart of a little child that makes it incredibly easy for them to share with others? I am not an expert on such things, but I think it comes down to their understanding of ownership. They don't really own anything. Sure, they have their security blanket that is theirs alone, but for the most part, everything else is fair game.

It is only when they grasp the concept of possessing and defending their own personal property that their generous hearts diminish. The smaller the child, the more foreign this concept of possession is. As far as they are concerned, they have all they need when they need it, so it is not necessary to hold on to anything too tightly.

Maybe that is what makes them so generous? What if we, as adults, could return to a place of such beautiful generosity that we would not feel the need to protect, withhold and barricade our own possessions like we do?

What if we were so convinced that we have infinite access to all of the riches in glory of heaven (Philippians 4:19) that we could freely give to others what we have freely received? Maybe that is why God loves a cheerful, hilarious giver? Maybe the smaller we become in our hearts, the less ownership will represent something we are afraid to lose?

I am not saying I have got this childlike attribute sorted out in my own life; I still drive my own car, live in my own house, etc. I am not at a place where if someone simply asks to use my cell phone, I would freely share it. However, I do find it intriguing to wonder if this is one of those beautiful characteristics of a childlike heart that truly makes little kids great in God's eyes?

I know I am asking more questions in this chapter than I have answers for, but these things are just food for thought. My prayer is that we would all be so convinced that our Papa will provide for all we need, when we need it, and that we will no longer need to have a hoarder mentality.

I pray God would release an overwhelming generosity through us that makes sharing with others the most fun game ever.

2 Corinthians 9:7
Let each man give according as he has determined in his heart; not grudgingly, or under compulsion; for God loves a cheerful giver (WEB).

-44-
LITTLE CHILDREN LOOK LIKE THEIR PARENTS

One of the joys of being a parent is that you see a reflection of yourself in your children. After all, God used your DNA as the building blocks to make them into the spectacular creation they have become.

And this very same principle works for grandparents too. I can't tell you how much it puts a smile on my face when a friend tells me my granddaughter looks just like me. Recently, one of my friends posted on Facebook that Riley was a 'mini me'.

Oftentimes, not only do they pick up a combination of physical traits from mom and dad, but their personality traits as well. My wife is gentle and quiet, and our oldest daughter Kristin is gentle and quiet. I, on the other hand, can be a little opinionated and rambunctious at times, and our youngest daughter Candice shares those same qualities. I consider our son Steve a mixture of both parents.

This is God's intended order of things. When He designed humanity's first couple and blessed them to be fruitful and multiply, He passed on their genetic code from one generation to the next. The basic principle of creation is 'like begets like' (Genesis 1:24-25). Apple trees bear apples; pear trees produce more pears. It would be completely unnatural and impossible for an orange tree to produce bananas. That is not how things work.

If we don't grasp this most basic (but most important) understanding, we will risk misunderstanding who we really are. If like begets like, what does God produce? Luke 3:38 tells us that Adam was the son of God. When we can really grasp the Godhead's intent for humanity in the garden, it will change the way we see ourselves.

I think this is why the theory of evolution is so devastating to the human heart. The idea that our origins came from apes instead of the divine strikes a blow to the heart of our true purpose. However, when we see that God's intent was that we would be a reflection of His own image on planet earth (Genesis 1:26-27), it elevates our position in creation to its true place.

An unshakeable reality of life is that only children can reveal and reflect who their parents really are. I can remember when our son Steve was a little boy, he liked to copy what I was doing. If I was sitting at a computer typing, he would grab a keyboard and type as well.

In the same way I gained my love for gadgets from my dad, Steve is a chip off the old block and is more of a tekkie than I could ever hope to be. That is how life is supposed to work. Sons look like their fathers.

We see this foundational principle at work in the life of Jesus in all He did while on earth. He was the image of the invisible God (Colossians 1:15) and the exact representation of His being (Hebrews 1:3). He reaffirmed this to His disciples in John 14:9: Jesus said to him, "Have I been with you such a long time, and do you not know me, Philip? He who has seen me has seen the Father. How do you say, 'Show us the Father?'" (WEB).

This is why it is so important for us to focus on learning to be a son or daughter to God rather than being preoccupied with our ministry gifts. If we are to be conformed into the image of the Son (Romans 8:29), it only stands to reason that we will reflect the same Spirit of Sonship (Galatians 4:6-7) that Jesus has. It is sons and daughters that the Father lavishes His love on, not ministry professionals.

If we keep our focus on the ministry gifts God has entrusted us with rather than our true identity as being His children, we will settle for an identity far inferior than that of being children of the Most High. The call of the Christian life is to be imitators of God as His dearly loved children (Ephesians 5:1). The Message translation says, "Watch what God does, and then you do it, like children who learn proper behavior from their parents" (MSG).

I believe one of the main reasons we struggle to live our Christian life to its full potential is that we don't know who we truly are. It is as if we are trying to live by a set of good values and guidelines, just like other religions have in place. But that, my friend, is not the good news Jesus Christ secured for us.

We are a new creation (2 Corinthians 5:17) with a brand new nature that is united with Christ in His royal position within the Trinity (John 17:23). We are no longer orphans (John 14:18) but co-heirs with Christ (Romans 8:17) and we are actually seated with Him on His throne in heavenly places (Ephesians 2:6).

Jesus' Father has become our Father (John 20:17) and as such, we are now active participants of His own divine nature (2

Peter 1:4). The New Covenant declares that the Father has implanted His own seed (Greek word - *sper'-mah*) in you because that is what fathers do (1 John 3:9).

The spiritual reality of God being your true Father (2 Corinthians 6:18) supersedes the natural reality of your earthly father. And it is amazing to think that as Jesus is, so are you in this world (1 John 4:17; Galatians 2:20).

My prayer is that the Spirit of Wisdom and Revelation would open the eyes of our hearts to see this game changing truth in action in our lives (Ephesians 1:17-23).

The truth is, we are no longer slaves and servants looking to appease a temperamental master. We are actually sons and daughters of Yahweh. It serves us and the world around us if we act like it.

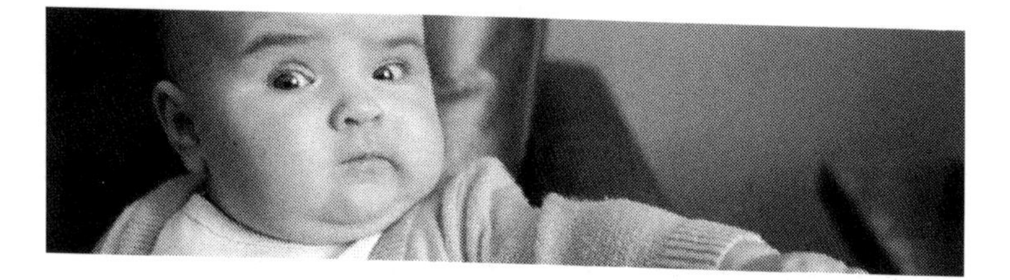

-45-
LITTLE CHILDREN AREN'T IMPRESSED WITH TITLES

I find it hilarious to watch when a little child comes in contact with someone who is really important. The adults around will change their behavior but the little kids don't. It doesn't matter to a child whether they are in the presence of the queen of England or any commoner; they treat them all the same.

And I love that about little kids. They are not a respecter of persons. They see everyone equally and do not judge or try to flatter in order to improve their social standing. They don't judge skin color, financial status, or the measurements of power and influence that an adult world pays deference to.

In many ways, they see people similar to how God sees them. While He loves all of us equally, He doesn't seem too impressed with our titles, wealth, strength or our social status. Romans 2:11 tells us that God does not show favoritism.

The systems of this world honor the elite while the Kingdom of God exalts the poor, the weak, the foolish and the childlike. If we don't see life through the lens of God's perspective, we will miss out on the high value He places on the disenfranchised and marginalized among us.

I think that is why we may pay lip service to becoming like little kids again, but in fact, we refuse to embrace all of the real wonders of being small. One of the last words of encouragement that Jack Winter gave to some of the folks attending a Father's Love Forum was, "Stay small in your own eyes."

Jack was referring to what made Saul qualified to serve as Israel's first king. In 1 Samuel 15:17, Samuel said, "Although you were once small in your own eyes, did you not become the head of the tribes of Israel? The Lord anointed you king over Israel"(NIV). The reality was that, physically, Saul was a head taller than anyone else in Israel, but spiritually, he was little in his heart. And it was that childlike humility that caused Yahweh to choose him as king.

If we stay small in our own eyes, our inflated egos won't get in the way of seeing the world as God sees it. When we look through the eyes of a little child, we won't show favoritism to the biggest and the brightest among us. If we keep small, we won't judge people based on a broken value system that God rejects.

In God's wonderful Kingdom, there is a level playing field. The strong are made low and the weak are exalted. Children are the greatest and the kings of the earth are humbled. True greatness is celebrated in the weak and the foolish. When we see the world as our Abba sees it, the disabled among us are considered true princes and princesses in the Kingdom of our God.

My prayer is that we would all be able to return to a vantage point where we stop seeing the world through adult eyes. May our Papa give us the grace to see the level playing field He has created where everyone is loved and celebrated equally in His sight.

-46-
LITTLE CHILDREN ARE GREAT RESPONDERS

Little kids are great responders. As a matter of fact, there is not much else they can do at the earliest age other than respond. They can't initiate feeding themselves or changing themselves. Nor are they responsible for any other necessities of life.

As they grow, they learn to respond more expressively. I can remember the first time we saw Riley smile back at us. We were absolutely thrilled that she was communicating in such a loving way to her grandparents.

I think this is a very important attribute of a childlike heart that will help us navigate our Father's Kingdom better. 1 John 4:19 is one of the shortest verses in the Bible, but I believe if we can put into practice what it says, we've got all we need to live a beautiful life. It simply says, "We love him, because he first loved us" (WEB).

Wow! Such simplicity. The Christian life is meant to be a life where God initiates His love and we respond in kind. That's it. If we get this one verse secure in our hearts, I believe we are good to go. Ungodly religion will try and teach us that we have to initiate good works to God in order to be loved and accepted by Him. Perhaps if we read the Bible front to back, it will be enough. But how much is enough?

Maybe if we increase our giving and our church attendance. Or maybe we need to fast weekly? Will that make us acceptable in God's sight? The good news Jesus secured for us is that it was His Father who did all of the initiating when He sent His only Son into the world two thousand years ago (John 3:16).

1 John 4:10 actually gives us a biblical definition of what love is when it says, "This is love: not that we loved God, but that he loved us and sent his Son as an atoning sacrifice for our sins" (NIV).

I believe the more we are able to embrace the simplicity of learning to live a life of responding to God's ongoing initiative of love, the more peace we will experience. When we finally realize that it has never been about us, we will be able to cease from our own works, relax and just sink into the goodness of God that is already in you.

No longer will we have to try to create new initiatives in hope that one day we might be worthy enough for love, because love has already made us worthy. That is good news for every broken and battered heart and something little kids intuitively expect from their parents.

I pray that you would prepare your heart to receive all of the love and goodness your Heavenly Father wants to shower on you. Not because you deserve it, but because your Dad is the very source of all love and He loves to continually pour out His affection into your heart by His Holy Spirit.

May Abba give you the grace to simply respond to His kindness.

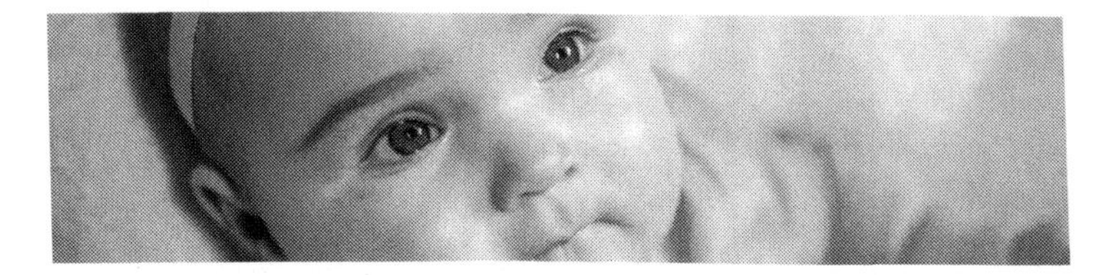

-47- LITTLE CHILDREN HAVE A SECURE INHERITANCE

My children will not have to strive or contend for their inheritance. It is theirs by virtue of their birthright. All that my wife and I have belongs to them simply because they are our children. This is how a healthy, loving family works. We receive inheritances from our parents and then in turn pass it on to our kids.

Even the smallest of babies in a family are considered future heirs of all that belongs in their generational line. The best example I can think of is the royal family in the United Kingdom. William and Kate currently have two children: Prince George and Princess Charlotte. Even though they really have no intellectual properties to contribute to the kingdom, they are already considered heirs to the throne.

In the same way these little ones are full-fledged members of royalty, so are we. Ephesians 1:13-14 says we have been given the Holy Spirit as a deposit to guarantee our inheritance. 2 Corinthians 1:22 says, "and he has identified us as his own by placing the Holy Spirit in our hearts as the first installment that guarantees everything he has promised us" (NLT).

The truth is, you can never work hard enough to earn an inheritance. It has to be freely given and the only qualifier is that you must belong to the family to get it. If we fail to understand this most basic principle in Father's family, we will spend a wasted life in search of an elusive blessing that is already ours in Christ.

How much does little George or Charlotte have to work to earn their position in the royal family? The obvious answer is they don't have to work for it because it is already theirs. If the answer is clear in the natural realm of royalty, why do we struggle so much to grasp this in the spiritual realm?

It is as if we think that there is a mystical merit system we have to abide by in order to be found worthy of an inheritance. The reality is that it simply does not exist. You are either born into the family or you are not. If you are not, come on in and receive God's free gift. If you are already in, there is nothing you could ever do to secure what is already yours.

Ephesians 2:8-9
8 for by grace you have been saved through faith, and that not of yourselves; it is the gift of God, 9 not of works, that no one would boast (WEB).

God has given us a gift of untold wealth. We could never earn it, deserve it or fight to keep it. It is part of the eternal inheritance package our Big Brother secured for us when He took our rightful place on the cross.

My prayer is that this life changing reality would become more than just a concept we acknowledge, but an honest to goodness reality that causes us to wake up to our royal position in Christ. Whether you are a newborn babe in Christ or an old geezer like me who has been in the Kingdom for over forty years, may all of our hearts be set at rest knowing we all have the same inheritance that Jesus has.

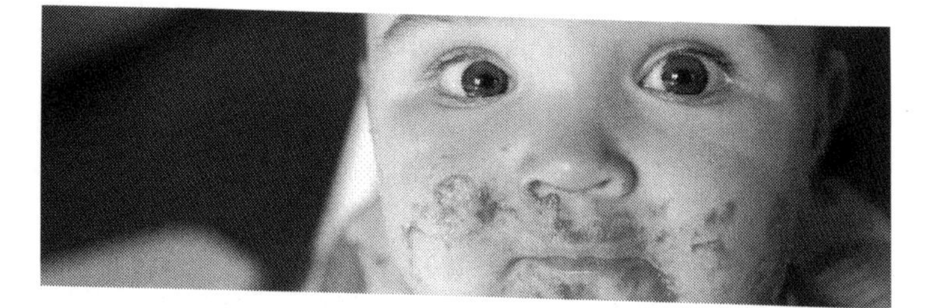

-48-
LITTLE CHILDREN CAN EAT ALL THE BREAD THEY WANT

In Matthew 15:22-28, there is a story about a Canaanite woman (a non Jew) who asked Jesus to heal her demonized daughter. Jesus said to her that it was not appropriate to give the children's bread to dogs. The mother responded by saying that even dogs get to eat the crumbs that fall from the table. Jesus was so impressed with her faith, He healed her daughter even though, at the time, His healing was reserved primarily for the Jews.

What I want to emphasize here is that Jesus says that *healing is the children's bread.* When our children were living at home, they had full and unrestricted access to our refrigerator. Of course they had to keep meals in mind so their snacking wouldn't affect their appetite, but in general, food was a basic right to them.

In the same way, Jesus is telling us that healing is a basic right for God's kids. And if healing is symbolized by bread, I think it is fairly safe to say we can ask the Father for our bread every day (Matthew 6:11). In Matthew 7:7-11, Jesus encourages His listeners to make their requests known to God. Keep asking. Keep seeking. Keep knocking. He tells them that even evil fathers give bread when their children ask for it, so how much more will your Father in heaven give good gifts?

So my encouragement for you is, if you need healing of any kind, don't be afraid to ask your Father for bread; it is a basic right for every son or daughter of Almighty God. Just like little kids can go to the kitchen to get bread when they are hungry, so we can go to God any time we need to for healing.

This is something we need to be mindful of every day now. Since our daughter was diagnosed with Leukemia, she has had to endure near daily chemotherapy treatments and she has nearly another year of daily treatments ahead of her. With every day that comes, our prayer to our Father on her behalf is 'Give us this day our daily bread.'

As we continue to walk alongside our daughter through her full recovery, we are mindful of those around us who are suffering as well. My prayer is that you would experience the nearness of God in the midst of your struggles and know in your heart that healing is the children's bread.

May you be comforted in knowing that you can partake of the unlimited supply of bread that comes from heaven any time you have a need.

John 6:32-35
32 Jesus therefore said to them, "Most certainly, I tell you, it wasn't Moses who gave you the bread out of heaven, but my Father gives you the true bread out of heaven. 33 For the bread of God is that which comes down out of heaven, and gives life to the world." 34 They said therefore to him, "Lord, always give us this bread." 35 Jesus said to them, "I am the bread of life. He who comes to me will not be hungry, and he who believes in me will never be thirsty (WEB).

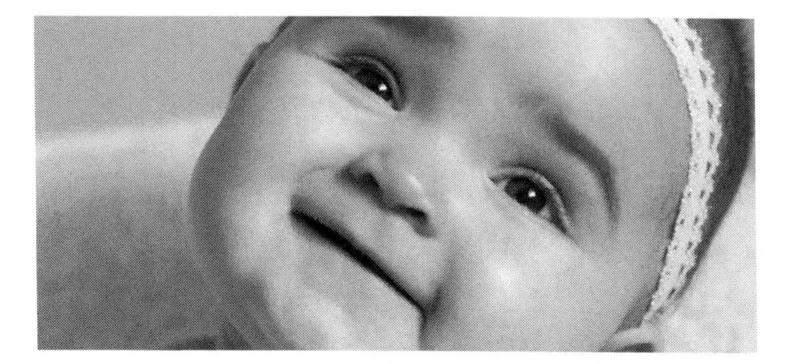

-49-
LITTLE CHILDREN HAVE ANGELS THAT SEE THE FATHER

I am convinced little children see into the supernatural realm far more than we realize. Over the years, I have heard many stories of little kids who have had angelic visitations and encounters with things far too big for an adult mind to comprehend. I think it is because they don't have an adult sized intellect that would nullify such divine encounters.

Good friends of ours have a young son who regularly has visions of Jesus in his bedroom. To him, it's no big deal because he assumes everybody else can see Jesus too. It makes me wonder how many children have encounters as little kids that they actually forget about when they get bigger?

In Matthew 18, Jesus takes quite a bit of time talking about the greatness of little kids. In verse 10, we read about how their personal angels are always beholding the face of the Father in heaven: See that you don't despise one of these little ones, for I tell you that in heaven their angels always see the face of my Father who is in heaven (WEB).

As far as I can recall, there is no place in the New Testament that makes such a clear cut statement about this kind of role of angels with grown ups. But for little kids and those with a childlike heart, their angels have a front row seat in the throne room.

I believe when we return to the place of childlike faith and wonder in our own hearts, it opens up a gateway for us to encounter more of the supernatural realm than we can comprehend with an adult mindset.

The story that comes to mind is in 2 Kings 6:8-23 where the prophet, Elisha, prayed that God would open up his servant's eyes to see the angelic protection that was surrounding them. Elisha didn't pray for angels to come, he simply prayed that this young man's inner eyes would be opened so he could see the chariots of fire that were already surrounding them in another dimension.

Little kids are far more in touch with their inner eyes than us adults are. They would have no problem believing that angels in chariots of fire were surrounding them just like they did with Elisha and that their personal angels represent them well in heaven.

May God give us the grace to see with our inner eyes too, so that we can be awakened to the supernatural Kingdom realm that is surrounding us at this very moment.

2 Kings 6:16-17
16 He answered, "Don't be afraid; for those who are with us are more than those who are with them." 17 Elisha prayed, and said, "Yahweh, please open his eyes, that he may see." Yahweh opened the young man's eyes; and he saw: and behold, the mountain was full of horses and chariots of fire around Elisha. (WEB).

-50-
LITTLE CHILDREN ARE LOVE SPONGES

Love is the substance that the human heart needs in order to thrive in life. Without love, little kids can develop physical and emotional disorders that will affect the way they relate to the world in which they live.

There is no 'love school' we can send our babies to that teaches them how to receive love. They simply expect it from the moment they are born. God has woven the need for love deep into the fabric of their beings and they are very comfortable in an atmosphere of love and affection.

Seldom will you ever see a little child in a healthy family be uncomfortable with love. Sure, there will be times when they are cranky and restless, but for the most part, a hug is always welcomed by little ones.

I would say that little kids are love sponges; they have the beautiful ability to soak in all of the love a person can give them. The more they receive, the more secure they become. They actually thrive in an atmosphere of love.

My wife and I are so blessed to be able to watch how our granddaughter Riley is reveling in the love she is growing up in. Whether it's from her loving parents, Nick and Kristin, or her uncles and aunts, Riley continues to be the center of every family gathering.

I am looking forward to seeing how this foundation of love will cause Riley to flourish in the days to come. Her ability to be a love sponge is a constant reminder of how my Papa wants me to live too.

A good friend of mine told me a story about an encounter he had with his own granddaughter when she was little. They were planning to watch a movie together, so they put on her favorite one and started watching it. A few minutes into the movie, the little girl asked her grandpa to put on another DVD because she said the second movie was her favorite.

After watching the second movie for a few minutes, she paused the DVD and asked for her grandpa to put on a third movie because that one was her favorite. By this time, my friend David, was a little bewildered at how his granddaughter could love so many movies and see them all as her favorites.

After all, in the mind of a grown up, you can only have one favorite. God spoke to him and said that his adult thinking was limiting his perspective. Adults think linearly and rationally about most things. Little kids are NOT limited to linear thinking, so from their perspective, they have no problem with the concept that every movie is their favorite.

It was funny because my friend heard God say that He didn't have those adult limitations either. As far as God is concerned,

He does not need to have only one favorite in His family. From His eternal non-linear view, each one of His kids is His favorite.

It is this kind of intense love that the Father has for each one of His children. He is not limited by our own adult view of how love should work and the pecking order we put people in. He loves us unconditionally and completely because He is the source of all love (1 John 4:16).

The truth is, we were all created to be loved unconditionally, and it is only when we make love our greatest aim that we will find what we were designed to experience (1 Corinthians 14:1).

I am pretty sure that at the end of my life, I will not be thinking about how much longer I should have worked at the office or how many more ministry trips I should have taken.

I believe the most important things to me at that holy moment will be the things that reduce me to love. My thoughts will be focused on who I loved and who loved me, because at the end of the day, it is only love that really matters.

I was able to tangibly experience God's priority of love in a way I had not yet known in the early days of Candice's diagnosis. My wife and I were scheduled to leave for a big trip to the UK just nine days after we discovered our daughter had Leukemia.

The plan was to fly home from the UK to drop my wife off, and then leave again for another two weeks of meetings with underground church leaders in an undisclosed location. It had taken a long time to set up these very important connections and I thought this trip was going to be the most significant ministry moment of my life.

We of course cancelled both trips so we could be at our

daughter's hospital bedside. At the end of a daylong hospital visit, I took a solitary walk to pick up my car. As I walked, I reflected on those trips, trying to grasp what all the planning was about only to have them cancelled.

I said to Papa, "I thought this trip to meet with the underground church was going to be the biggest ministry moment of my life." Further imprinting on my heart what He considers to be the highest priority, He answered with the words, "Being at your daughter's bedside is the biggest ministry moment of your life."

In that moment, I saw in a far more profound way than ever before how important it is for me to be a father to my children. For when I stand in the role of a father, I am representing the love of my Abba and that is something He takes very seriously.

I truly believe that our greatest achievements will pale in comparison to the priority of love we express to both our natural and spiritual family. 1 Corinthians 13:1-3 reminds us that even the greatest ministry accomplishments are completely empty when love isn't present.

1 If I speak with the languages of men and of angels, but don't have love, I have become sounding brass, or a clanging cymbal. 2 If I have the gift of prophecy, and know all mysteries and all knowledge; and if I have all faith, so as to remove mountains, but don't have love, I am nothing. 3 If I dole out all my goods to feed the poor, and if I give my body to be burned, but don't have love, it profits me nothing (WEB).

Being a husband, a dad, a son and a grandpa are my highest priorities these days. Whether I ever decide to travel internationally again or not, I believe when I manifest God's love to those closest to me, I am truly being a reflection of the family love that was lost in the garden.

May God give all of us the grace to do everything in love (1 Corinthians 16:14), so we can learn to be as comfortable with love as little kids are.

For the life changing truth that will indeed transform us from glory to glory is that God not only loves us throughout eternity, but He is loving us in this very moment.

John 15:9
Even as the Father has loved me, I also have loved you. Remain in my love (WEB).

-51- APOSTLES OF LOVE

The Apostle John is known as the apostle of love. With the exception of the Book of Revelation, all his other writings seem to focus on the priority of love that is found within the Godhead. In the gospel account he himself wrote, he doesn't even refer to himself by name. He refers to himself as "the disciple whom Jesus loved."

So it should be no surprise this revelation of love that John carried caused him to reveal a far more intimate description of Jesus' relationship with His Father than the other three gospels did. He was present to hear Jesus' high priestly prayer in John 17 and he was the only disciple who stayed with Jesus until the very end.

From reading his gospel narrative, I think it is fair to say his writings revealed that he was Jesus' best friend and his closest confidant. Even when Jesus hung on the cross, it was his best friend John that was entrusted with the care of Jesus' mom for the rest of her life (John 19:25-27).

There is a story told in church tradition about how this great apostle was reduced to the simplicity of love in his old age.

While being carried around by his disciples in Ephesus, it is said that John would give them this one charge over and over again, "Little children, love one another."

As his disciples grew tired of the repetitive nature of this one statement, they asked him why it was necessary for him to keep repeating himself. Church tradition tells us that his response was simple and to the point, "It is the Lord's command. And if this alone be done, it is enough." [9]

In the great love letter John wrote that we call 1 John, he addresses his audience as little children on nine separate occasions. I don't think it is any coincidence that one of the greatest books in the Bible that talks about God's love, also talks about us being little children. For it is only when we are able to open up our hearts to the Father as His little ones, that we will truly be able to receive His fatherly affection in its purest form.

From my own personal experience, I consider Jack Winter to be one of Abba's apostles of love to me. It was through Jack's life and his loving embrace that this broken hearted little boy found home. In the short time I knew Jack, I learned so much about how to be a little boy with a big Dad.

In the last private meeting I was at with leaders of the Father's Love Forum, his charge to us was "Stay small in your own eyes." In the last public meeting I ever heard him speak at, Jack echoed the words of the Apostle John as he gently encouraged us with the words, "Little children, love one another."

A few months later, Jack would complete his journey home to his Father's house. I will never forget the last words he said to me as I was leaving his house after saying one last goodbye to him.

I was at his front door on my way to the airport. I turned my head to wave goodbye one last time and from a distance, I heard him say the words "love you" to me. Those words, beyond any other words I heard him say, still resonate in the deepest place in my being.

At the end of my life, I hope I will be reduced to love, just like John and Jack were.

-52- LEARNING TO 'GROW DOWN'

The older I get, the more value I see in embracing a childlike heart. The reality is, I don't have to try to be a little boy that needs to be loved. I AM a little boy who needs to be loved. And my Heavenly Papa is continuing to love me right now.

This is the very place my Father met me over seventeen years ago when Jack Winter wrapped his arms around me. And being a little boy who needs to be loved continues to be the place where I meet my Abba whenever I feel like I have no strength to run my race.

The place where I encounter my Dad's love the most is at the times when I feel I least deserve it. I think the reason this is the case is because there are lingering remnants of the orphan boy that still remain who thinks love is something to be earned. So in times when I would expect rejection rather than His affirmation, Papa is continuing to love the orphan right out of me.

There have been many occasions in this journey when I have tried to grow up again in order to be accepted and understood by the adult world around me. But each time I do, I discover that I am simply not equipped to run with the big boys because after all, I'm just little. It is only when I return to the safe place of being helpless and dependent on my Dad that I find solace in the midst of a world that would want me to be more than I am.

Earlier in this book, I mentioned that Jack Winter said we are just three year olds teaching two year olds. I honestly don't think I'm that big yet, but I am certainly comfortable to live in that neighborhood.

If you think I am living in denial because of my refusal to grow up, please be kind and leave me alone because it is working! In this beautiful place of being carried on my Father's shoulders, my wife and I have experienced countless adventures that would have never been possible in our own strength.

Staying little has helped me manage the impossible vision of wanting to deliver the Father's Love Letter to every person on the planet. Staying little has helped me manage the public demands of ministry and the millions of visitors we have had on our websites over the years.

Staying little has protected me from trying to compete in a grown up ministry world where there are so many dear folks that are so much more competent and gifted than me. Staying little keeps my heart in a place of rest and peace knowing that my life is enough the way God made me.

Staying little has helped free me from the unrealistic expectations of others, so I can simply be the unique, one-of-a-kind work of art that Papa intended for me. In this place of staying small in my own eyes, I have found a haven of contentment where I no longer need to prove myself over and over again to those who demand more than I can give.

Staying little has even sustained my wife and I in the darkest times, walking alongside our daughter during her cancer treatment. Staying little has helped calm my fears in the times when I have felt absolutely overwhelmed and vulnerable.

Papa has even encouraged me to return to a time in my life when I loved to draw, and together we created a cartoon series in the cancer clinic. These precious times with my Dad have proven to be an unexpected source of joy and comfort in the face of some pretty daunting circumstances.

And last but not least, staying little has helped me appreciate just how important it is for me to belong to Abba's family. Being a little boy with a really big Dad has helped me see, in a new way, that the common denominator of the human heart is our foundational need for family love.

I am learning that the good news of the gospel is simply inviting people to return to God's intended purpose for them as His beloved children. In light of humanity's foundational need for family love, I believe evangelism is simply the process in which we point orphans towards home.

I believe when people really make the connection between their need for family love and the source of all family love (which is in the embrace of the Trinity), something familiar will resonate in the very core of their being.

It is when people truly discover that their very existence was birthed in the heart of a loving Father before the foundation of the world that their hearts will truly be awakened to the family love they were created to experience (Ephesians 1:3-6).

Home is what we were created for and home is where we all belong. The prodigal son turned his heart towards home when he was in need.

May God give us the wisdom to be able to help people in every culture get in touch with their foundational need to be loved so we can simply point their hearts toward home.

I am so thankful that Jesus Christ, the Son of the living God, became the way in which we could find our way home (John 14:1-6). Home to the family love we were created to experience and home to our divine destiny as Yahweh's beloved kids.

If the Kingdom does belong to little children like Jesus says it does, then this is where I want to live the rest of my life. I am learning that being a little boy with a really BIG Dad is the only place where I can be small enough to be able to contain the immeasurable vastness of My Father's Kingdom. My hope and prayer is that you would join me there too.

As Jack Winter used to say, "The smaller that we can become, the bigger that our Father can become on our behalf."

Mark 10:13-16
13 They were bringing to him little children, that he should touch them, but the disciples rebuked those who were bringing them. 14 But when Jesus saw it, he was moved with indignation, and said to them, "Allow the little children to come to me! Don't forbid them, for God's Kingdom belongs to such as these. 15 Most certainly I tell you, whoever will not receive God's Kingdom like a little child, he will in no way enter into it." 16 He took them in his arms, and blessed them, laying his hands on them (WEB).

THE BEST DAD IN THE UNIVERSE

When children are little, they are happy to boast about their dads... how big they are... how strong they are... I remember my kids boasted about me that way when they were small. It really touched my heart so see them think of me in that way.

'My Dad Is The Best Dad In The Universe' is my best attempt to boast in the same way about my Heavenly Father. Each line is inspired by a Bible text, over 150 in total!

If the Father's Love Letter was Abba's way of reaching out to me, then this is my way of responding back to him! I hope it is a blessing to you…

My Dad is the best Dad in the universe (Psalm 113:5) and the Father over all creation (Ephesians 4:4-6).

He is so amazing, that He clothes Himself with light (Psalm 104:2) and He rides on the wings of the wind (Psalm 104:3).

My Dad is so powerful that He created the heavens and the earth (Genesis 1:1) with just the sound of His voice (Genesis 1:3).

He made all the stars in the sky (Job 9:9) and He calls each one of them by name (Psalm 147:4).

My Dad is so big, heaven is His throne room and the earth is His footstool. (Isaiah 66:1)

When my Dad speaks, His voice roars like thunder (Job 37:5) and flashes like lightning (Psalm 29:7). His hair is white like wool and He sits on a throne of fire (Daniel 7:9).

Some call Him the Ancient of Days (Isaiah 43:13) because He has been around forever (Psalm 90:2) but I just call Him my Dad because He said He would be a Father to me. (2 Corinthians 6:18)

My Dad knows everything about everything from the beginning to the end (Isaiah 46:10).

When He opens up His hand, He provides for all that He created (Psalm 145:16).

Everything that my Dad makes is really good (Genesis 1:31). He invented every bird, every fish, and every animal that ever lived (Genesis 1:20-22) and He gives life and breath to all things (Acts 17:24-25).

All of creation is constantly speaking about My Dad's kindness (Romans 1:20).

The heavens show off His glory and the skies display His majesty (Psalm 19:1).

My Dad is so huge, He holds the entire earth in the palm of His hand (Psalm 95:4).

Some call Him Creator because of what He makes (Isaiah 40:28), but I just call Him my Dad, because He loves me with all His heart (1 John 3:1).

My Dad is so rich, The entire earth belongs to Him (Psalm 24:1). He even owns the cattle on a thousand hills (Psalm 50:10).

Though nations tremble in His presence (Psalm 99:1), I call Him my Father (John 16:25-27).

Though the angels bow down in reverence (Revelation 7:11), I can come into His throne room any time, night or day (Hebrews 4:16).

My Dad's kingdom is really really big (Psalm 145:13). It is always expanding and it will last forever (Isaiah 9:7).

My Dad rules the nations of the world and all the kings belong to Him (Psalm 47:7-9).

His righteousness towers like the mountaintops and His justice goes deep as the sea (Psalm 36:6).

My Dad is the kindest person in the universe (Deuteronomy 7:9).

He sends His rain and sunshine on both the good and the bad (Matthew 5:45).

He loves to show mercy (Ephesians 2:4) even when we don't deserve it (Romans 5:8) because His great love endures forever (1 Chronicles 16:34).

My Dad's love stretches to the heavens and His faithfulness extends beyond the clouds (Psalm 36:5).

He is the most gentle (2 Samuel 22:36), the most forgiving (1 John 1:9), the most compassionate (Lamentations 3:22-23) and most understanding Dad in the universe (Psalm 103:13-14).

He is always the same (Malachi 3:6). He never changes His mind (Numbers 23:19) and He always keeps His Word (Isaiah 55:10-11).

Every promise He makes is true (Hebrews 10:23) and the intentions of His heart will stand forever (Psalm 33:11).

My Dad's heart is for the underdog (1 Corinthians 1:26-29).

He protects the weak (Isaiah 40:29) and He has chosen the poor of this world to inherit His kingdom (James 2:5).

He cares for the fatherless and the widow (Jeremiah 49:11). He isn't happy when people do evil things and He rejoices when justices wins out (1 Corinthians 13:6).

My Dad is an Everlasting Father (Isaiah 9:6) who is always present to help me when I need Him (Psalm 46:1).

He is my safe place in times of trouble (Nahum 1:7). He is my strong tower (Proverbs 18:10) and He lifts up my head when I get discouraged (Psalm 3:3).

My Dad knew me even before I was conceived (Jeremiah 1:5). He actually chose me before the foundation of the world (Ephesians 1:4-5).

He formed me with His own hands (Psalm 119:73) when He knit me together in my mother's womb (Psalm 139:13).

My Dad created me to look just like Him (Genesis 1:27) and He says that I am fearfully and wonderfully made (Psalm 139:14).

The day I was born, my Dad was in the delivery room to welcome me into this world (Psalm 71:6) because I am the apple of His eye (Psalm 17:8) and the object of His affection (John 17:23).

No one can hurt me because my Dad fights for me (Exodus 14:14). He even sends His angels to watch over me (Psalm 91:11).

Nothing can harm me when I stay close to Him (Psalm 91:9-10).

Because my Dad is for me, no one can stand against me (Romans 8:31).

My Dad is really, really patient (1 Corinthians 13:4). He is not proud or rude or self-centered, and He does not get mad easily (1 Corinthians 13:5).

He does not keep track of all the times I hurt Him (1 Corinthians 13:5), and He loves to forgive and forget (Hebrews 8:12).

My Dad always protects, He always trusts, He always hopes for the best. My Dad will never give up on me (1 Corinthians 13:7) because His love will never fail (1 Corinthians 13:8).

Even if my earthly mom could forget, my Heavenly Dad will never forget me (Isaiah 49:15-16).

He understands everything about me (Psalm 139:1-3) and He knows what I need before I even ask (Matthew 6:8).

Every day in my life was written in His special book before one of them ever came to be (Psalm 139:16).

My Dad tells me all the time that I was created for His pleasure (Revelation 4:11) and that my life makes Him smile (Numbers 6:25).

He even took the time to number each one of the hairs of my head (Matthew 10:30).

My Dad loves to sing songs over me (Zephaniah 3:17) and He calls me His treasured possession (Deuteronomy 7:6).

He watches over me day and night because He never sleeps (Psalm 121:3).

My Dad has planned so many good things for me they are too many to count (Psalm 40:5).

He loves to share His secrets with me (Psalm 25:14) and He likes to show me the mysteries of His kingdom (Matthew 13:11).

My Dad likes to give good gifts too (Matthew 7:11).

Every gift I receive comes from His hand (James 1:17) and He keeps on telling me to ask Him for more (Matthew 7:7) because He delights to give me His kingdom (Luke 12:32).

When I get hurt, He heals me (Jeremiah 30:17). When I need reassurance, He comforts Me (2 Corinthians 1:3-4), just like a mother would (Isaiah 66:13).

When I feel weighed down, He carries all my burdens (Psalm 68:19).

When I am broken hearted, He is really, really close to me (Psalm 34:18).

My Dad is always with me (Isaiah 41:10) and He has promised to never leave me (Hebrews 13:5).

Even if I wanted to, there is no where I could go to ever leave His presence (Psalm 139:7-12).

When I fall, He picks me up (Psalm 37:24). When I am hurting, He encourages me (Psalm 10:17).

When I sin, He forgives me (Micah 7:18). When I can't go on, He carries me (Isaiah 46:4). When I lose faith, He doesn't give up on me (2 Timothy 2:13).

He gives me wisdom when I need it (James 1:5) and help when I'm in trouble (Psalm 46:1).

My Dad is always thinking of me (Psalm 139:17-18). He has really great plans in store for me (Jeremiah 29:11) and His heart is full of blessings towards me (Ephesians 1:3).

He holds me in the palm of His hand (John 10:29). He leads me to still waters and He gives rest to my soul (Psalm 23:2-3).

My Dad's patience astounds me (1 Timothy 1:16) and His mercy overwhelms me (Psalm 103:8).

His humility humbles me (Matthew 23:11) and His protecting wings cover me (Psalm 91:4).

His everlasting love sustains me (Jeremiah 31:3) and His provision keeps me (Matthew 6:25-26).

My cup overflows because of His kindness (Psalm 23:5), and mercy and goodness follow me wherever I go (Psalm 23:6).

When I was lost, My Dad found me (Luke 15). When I was mired in sin, He forgave me (1 John 1:9).

When I was filthy, He cleansed me (Hebrews 9:22).

When I was dead, He resurrected me (Romans 6:5).

When I was His enemy, He sent His only Son to die for me (Romans 5:10).

My Dad loved me so much (John 3:16) He gave up everything He loved in order to have my love (Romans 8:32).

Jesus Christ, the Son whom the Father loved (John 17:24) and the expressed image of the invisible God (Colossians 1:15) gladly became the Lamb slain before the foundation of the world (Revelation 13:8) so His Dad could be my Dad too (John 20:17).

Now, because of Jesus' death and resurrection (Romans 6:4-6) everything that belongs to Jesus belongs to me (Romans 8:15-17).

His joy is my joy (John 17:13). His peace is my peace (John 14:27). His life is my life (Galatians 2:20). His Dad is my Dad (Matthew 5:48).

He has given me the keys of the kingdom (Matthew 16:19) and He has made me an heir of His Father's inheritance (Galatians 4:6-7).

I am now part of the greatest family in the universe (Ephesians 3:14-15).

God is my Father (Psalm 68:5) and Jesus is my big brother (Hebrews 2:11).

They have even given me their own Spirit as a deposit to guarantee my inheritance (2 Corinthians 1:21-22).

My Dad has the biggest house ever and He has made a special room just for me (John 14:2-3), where I will rule and reign with Jesus forever (Revelation 22:5) in His unshakeable kingdom (Hebrews 12:28).

I have an everlasting inheritance in heaven waiting for me (1 Peter 1:3-4) where I will receive a crown of glory that will never fade (1 Peter 5:4).

One day, I will shine like the sun in my Father's kingdom (Matthew 13:43).

My Dad is so big, heaven can't contain Him (2 Chronicles 2:5-6) yet He is so small, He lives in my heart (John 14:23).

I am so glad that I will belong to His amazing family forever (John 8:35).

My Dad really is the BEST Dad in the universe!

2 Corinthians 6:18
And, "I will be a Father to you, and you will be my sons and daughters, says the Lord Almighty" (NIV).

To watch the video version, visit TheBestDad.net

ON THE LIGHTER SIDE…

One of the tangible benefits I have experienced when I discovered God loves me for who I am is the freedom to just be me. That may sound like I am stating the obvious when I say that, but the truth is many people wrestle with this same issue.

I grew up in a home where the priority to please people was considered a very noble personality trait. The only problem with that is when there are multiple people in the room, who do you try and please first?

This hamster wheel of trying to make everybody happy is absolutely brutal and the reality is, you will never be able to satisfy everybody's expectations all of the time. Since this has always been a really big part of my value system, I have found it extremely difficult to navigate the shark filled waters of trying to make people happy.

Over the years, I have visited every continent (with the exception of Antarctica) and I have bumped into many unrealistic expectations of what a traveling itinerant Fatherheart guy should be like. In order to dismantle any false expectations of me being larger than life, I have in some settings tried to strike a deathblow to them by telling a few unusual stories about my life.

I am sure I have offended some dear people in the process but I have not meant to. The truth is I am not a spiritual giant or some influential leader in the Kingdom. I am and will always be just a little boy who found home. Nothing more. Nothing less.

So in keeping in the same spirit of what I do in meetings, I want to share a bit of my life with you. I will apologize in advance to every person who might see these stories as unnecessary or frivolous. I have no interest in causing you any discomfort. All I want to do is lighten things up a bit and share my own weird and wacky life with those who might need a little chuckle or two.

You see, throughout my life, I have experienced some pretty embarrassing moments. On many occasions, I have asked the Lord to give me some insight into why all of these crazy things have happened to me. The only thing I have ever come up with is that God has chosen the foolish things of the world to confound the wise (1 Corinthians 1:26-29) so if that is the case, I qualify!

The thing is, I think my Heavenly Dad likes the way I am. In one of my stories, I got locked in a church bathroom when I was supposed to be the main speaker for the morning service. Nobody knew where I was because I had sneaked out during the worship time to have a bathroom break. The worship team had to keep playing until I was finally able to escape the clutches of the bathroom through an emergency exit and find my way back to the front of the church.

As I sat down, all of my embarrassing moments flashed before my eyes and I heard God chuckle and say to me, "Barry, I get a kick out of you!" So though I have no sound theological reasons for the bizarre things that happen to me, at least I can say I make my Dad smile.

At one meeting in California, a friend of mine was prophetically speaking to every person in the room. When it was my turn, my friend looked at me and said, "The Father says you are a space case!" Can you imagine God calling you a space case in a prophetic word? Well, at least I am His space case so I didn't mind in the least.

May these stories bring a lightness to your heart and a smile to your face. If nothing else, may they bring some comfort to you knowing that you are not me!

The need to categorize my embarrassing moments…

I have had so many embarrassing moments that I have needed to categorize them so I could keep track. I've created categories like outdoor, indoor, business and ministry moments to name just a few.

I stopped counting when I hit the fifty mark and there are many I simply am not able to share because they are way too embarrassing. I have fallen down stairs. I have fallen up stairs. I have been knocked out by a golf ball and knocked unconscious running into a concrete wall. I have chased a bear and had the same bear chase me. I have had birds, on more than one occasion, take a nosedive into my head and I have endured embarrassing moments on every continent I have ever visited.

Since time, space and my own reputation would prevent me from sharing all of them, I've decided to share just a few of the less embarrassing ones so you can better understand the wonderful and wacky adventures of a little boy that knows he is loved just the way he is.

Of course, names and places may be altered just a bit in order to protect the dignity of those who might have unintentionally been caught up in one of my events. Keep in mind I am not able to share my top ten, as they are far too embarrassing. :)

The Coffee Run

As a proud Canadian, I am very passionate about coffee. We even have a national coffee chain of stores that has embedded itself into our national identity. One of my moments involved this national coffee shop.

We had just finished a meeting at a church in Winnipeg, Manitoba and I asked my friend who was driving a mini van if he could stop for a moment so I could run in and get a coffee. My friend does not drink coffee, so he does not appreciate my addiction (*ahem*, I mean, my *enjoyment* of coffee), but he reluctantly agreed.

He was a little bit agitated and seemed to be in a hurry to get to the home we were being billeted at. As I opened the sliding door to run into the coffee shop, he was yelling at me to hurry up. In an effort to calm my friend's nerves, I ran as fast as I could there and back again.

I can remember holding two large coffees in my hand as I was running at breakneck speed to get back to the van. My friend yelled at me again to hurry up so I sped up my pace and leapt into the open sliding door of the van. I'm not the tallest person around but I still need to duck my head to get into the back seat of a van. The thing is though, I forgot to duck and I hit my head on the top part of the door as I landed in the van.

Now I found myself teetering with my toes in the van and my heels perilously floating outside of it. I knew I was about to fall backwards and I had a choice to make: drop the coffees and save myself, or hold onto the coffees and see what happens.

I decided to hold onto my beloved large coffees and let come what may. I ended up falling backwards out of the van, just like a tree falls in the forest, and I found myself lying on the sidewalk of the busy street with both arms stretched to the max holding up my coffees.

The good news is I didn't even spill one drop. The bad news was my friend wasn't even the least bit impressed with my antics and said to me, "Barry, stop messing around and get back into the van."

The Lunch Plate Sweep

I often get into trouble when I am overly preoccupied with trying to make a good impression on someone. I can remember one specific lunch meeting that I attended at a newspaper advertising executive's national meeting.

I was sitting beside one of the newspaper executives that intimidated me the most. He didn't smile much, wore an expensive suit and was a pretty big guy. Since I was one of the youngest guys in this organization, I wanted to make a good impression on him.

I thought I would do that best by trying to maintain eye contact with him while we ate our meal. To this day, I can remember very clearly what was on the menu: A pork chop, mashed potatoes, corn and lots of gravy.

At one point in our conversation, I was giving my best effort to try and separate the meat of the pork chop from the bone, all while maintaining eye contact with my associate. No matter how hard I tried, the meat wouldn't separate, so I had no choice but to increase the pressure. Then it happened.

The meat did in fact release from the bone but when it gave way, my knife swept across my plate sending the entire content of my pork chop, mashed potatoes, corn and gravy squarely onto the lap of this man's thousand dollar suit.

He didn't say a thing. He just looked down at his lap and stared at me in disbelief. It is in moments like this that words fail to express anything that could make up for what I had just done.

Chamber of Commerce Plate Stack

I became an executive in the newspaper business in my early thirties, so I always found myself a part of community organizations surrounded by municipal and business leaders who were much older than me.

To compensate for my youth, I always tried to put my best foot forward. One of the organizations I was a part of was our local Chamber of Commerce board of directors. Once a month, we would meet for a working lunch where we would discuss all of the important matters of business that affected our local community.

We held our meetings around a very large boardroom table so you could see everyone face to face. At one of these meetings, I arrived first and helped myself to the complimentary sandwiches, veggies and dip provided. I put it all on a stackable paper plate and found my seat.

Sometimes I can get into trouble when my overactive mind is in hyper-drive and I don't pay attention to what I am doing. This was one of those times. It was as if my thought life had brought me to another world, so I was oblivious to the rest of the business and community leaders that had joined the meeting.

All of a sudden my attention turned to the meeting and I noticed all of my esteemed colleagues were fumbling around trying to eat their sandwich, veggies and dip on napkins and not on the paper plates. I thought it was strange they wouldn't use the plates, as it was quite messy.

Then I looked down at my plate and realized the reason why they weren't using the paper plates. I didn't just take one of the plates. I'd grabbed the entire stack of plates to secure my single sandwich.

Even though no one said a word to me about it, it was obvious that all eyes were fixed me as I had my sandwich placed nicely on a stack of plates that looked like a mini tower of Babel. At this point, there was really no way for me to recover.

Virgin Caesar Tray Tip

When I was working in the newspaper business, I didn't drink alcohol, which made me the center of many jokes from my co-workers. Every time we went out for a business function, my drink of choice was a virgin Caesar, which was a tomato juice like beverage.

One time during a business lunch, I ordered my usual virgin Caesar. When the server brought it to the table, there was a celery stick protruding out of it that looked like a small tree. My colleagues laughed as the server (who I knew from my school days) brought it over to me.

I was feeling a little bit self-conscious at the time because we were in a restaurant and I felt like every eye was on me as I was getting served this 'girly man' drink. In an effort to speed up the serving process, I decided to take my drink off the tray before the server was prepared to give it to me. That day, I learned a very important lesson in what *not* to do when you are trying to be helpful to a waiter. Taking one drink off a full tray of drinks, without any notice to the server, put in motion a chain of events ending in all of the glasses falling off the tray.

To make matters worse, in an effort to rebalance the tray, I placed my massive virgin Caesar back on the tray to only see it tip over and spill all over my schoolmate's pristine white shirt. From top to bottom, the red tomato juice covered his once white uniform. Again, words failed to fix this awkward situation.

Mall Wall Crash

One day I was late for my hair cut appointment at a downtown mall in our city. Running at full speed towards the glass doors, trying to navigate which door I would choose all while watching carefully over my coffee.

There was a construction crew just outside of the mall who had stopped their work for a coffee break. In what seemed like the twinkling of an eye, I became distracted by these guys and instead of choosing the push door to enter the mall, I chose to enter through a solid pane of glass instead.

It was like the sound of a bird hitting a window, only with the sound and impact of a 200-pound man doing the same thing. My coffee exploded against the glass wall. Thankfully, the only thing that was bruised that day was my ego.

Of course, I couldn't bear to face these construction workers who were looking at me with blank stares, so I pretended nothing was wrong, found the door and went through like nothing ever happened.

Nice To Meet You 'Fluffy'

Whenever I visit a new home, I want to ensure that I make the children of the family I am staying with, feel important. On one particular occasion, with only a couple of hours sleep, I boarded a long flight to England.

When I arrived at my friend Mark's house, some of his family were there at the front door to greet me. Of course I did my best to make the children feel special and shook their hands and introduced myself.

After chatting a bit, I went into their living room and saw a young teenage girl sitting on the sofa. I shook her hand, introduced myself and asked what her name was. She didn't look too impressed as she said, "You just met me when you came in the front door." So much for making every child feel valued, eh?

In an effort to try to undo my faux pas, I asked her dad how I could get in her good books again. He said while her name was Francis, she liked to be called 'Flossie'. And if I were to call her Flossie, it would help me get out of the hole I'd dug for myself.

The next day, I was getting ready to speak at my friend's church and Flossie was standing with the other worship team members. I thought I would go up to her and call her by her nickname. So in front of all her friends, I warmly greeted her by saying, "Good to see you again, 'Fluffy'."

Windshield Washer Bullseye

While a friend of mine was visiting from England, I wanted to be hospitable and show him the area we lived in. It was a very cold January day and we were sitting in the car watching the sun go down.

It was a pretty spectacular sunset and my friend wanted to capture the moment with his camera. Unfortunately, my windshield was dirty so he couldn't take a good photo unless I cleaned it.

Everything happened in super slow motion. After my friend said he wanted to take a photo, I pressed the windshield washer button to clean the windshield. At the same time, he opened the door of my car to get out of the car to snap a shot.

As he poked his head in front of the car with his camera, the windshield washer squirter was activated and hit him square in his eye. While I was trying to be helpful, my friend didn't think I helped him much in the end.

Bubbles In A Gym

When our oldest daughter announced she was going to get married, I decided I was going to get a gym membership in order to lose a little weight before the big day. I signed up at the largest state of the art gym in our area.

My equipment of choice was an elliptical cross trainer. I used this one piece of equipment for sixty to ninety minutes every day, and had mastered the art of pushing and pulling with one hand, while the other hand navigated my phone.

I was able to answer email, surf the web, watch videos and so much more for the entire time I worked out each day. I was literally drenched with sweat after each work out but was happy to be making good progress towards my weight loss goals.

I had two pairs of shorts I liked to use every day. A spandex pair that served as the inside shorts and a regular pair that were on the outside. Since there was no way my wife could keep up with the laundry, I volunteered to hand wash both pairs of shorts every day after my workout and drip-dry them.

After a particularly sweaty workout session where I was totally immersed in my phone, I decided to step off the elliptical trainer. At that moment, I really didn't have a grid that would prepare me for what I would see next. There were bubbles completely surrounding both of my legs from my thigh to my knees!

And then I looked up and there were bubbles floating through the air in the gym. Can you imagine people's thoughts in the gym that morning? Here's this guy, exercising like a madmen, completely immersed in his phone, generating bubbles throughout the gym!

I went home and told my wife what happened and I asked her how in the world that could have happened. She asked me what detergent I used to wash the shorts and I told her I used dish/hand washing soap. Of course, she then told me that I wasn't supposed to use that kind of soap because it generates a lot of bubbles.

I guess the soap combined with lots of moisture and the agitation provided by two pairs of shorts moving back and forth created the ideal scenario for me to become a human washing machine!

So much more…

I have mistakenly driven a car on a bicycle path and through a carnival midway in Holland, stepped into an open manhole, and have been rescued from the clutches of a psychotic cat by a dear elderly lady who was working as a animal humane society volunteer. And of course, there are the top ten stories that I am not able (or willing) to share :)

Through all the weird and wacky things I have experienced in my life, I know one thing for sure: My Heavenly Father created me the way I am and He loves me through and through. Whether I am leaping tall buildings at a single bound or I am taking a nap, I am loved completely. And so are you.

I pray that you would find the freedom in your Heavenly Father's embrace to simply be the little boy or little girl He created you to be as well. For it is in the glorious simplicity of *living loved* that we will truly experience the time of our lives, enjoying life under the shadow of our Papa's wing.

So chill out, have lots of fun and stay little!

BIBLIOGRAPHY

1 Olympic athlete Derek Redmond - https://en.wikipedia.org/wiki/Derek_Redmond

2 The story of Rick and Dick Hoyt – TeamHoyt.com

3 NASA Creativity Test - (Source: George Land and Beth Jarman, Breaking Point and Beyond. San Francisco: HarperBusiness, 1993)

4 TEDx Tucson December 2011 Event
The Failure Of Success – Dr. George Land

5 Albert Einstein Quote - Cosmic Religion: With Other Opinions and Aphorisms (1931).

6 Spurgeon, Charles Haddon. "Commentary on Psalms 131:1". "Spurgeon's Verse Expositions of the Bible"

7 The Practise of the Presence of God – By Brother Lawrence

8 C.S. Lewis, Letters to Malcolm: Chiefly on Prayer (San Diego: Harvest, 1964), 92-93.

9 The Search for the Twelve Apostles book by William Steuart McBirnie Ph.D, Tyndale House 2008

Strong's Exhaustive Concordance - James Strong (1890), The Exhaustive Concordance of the Bible, Cincinnati: Jennings & Graham

ABOUT THE AUTHOR

After being hugged by a man named Jack Winter, Barry came into a life changing revelation that Almighty God was really his Dad. In response to this encounter with the love of God, he created a sermon illustration called Father's Love Letter.

Never in his wildest dreams did he imagine that this simple sermon illustration (first presented in January 1999) would end up being translated into 100+ languages, touching the hearts of many people around the world.

Barry & his wife Anneliese Adams have three grown children and one grandchild. They founded Father Heart Communications in 2000 to facilitate their mandate to simply point people's hearts towards home using the spoken word and every available technology on the Internet. Their main websites are fathersloveletter.com, 365promises.com and Fatherheart.tv

Made in the USA
Charleston, SC
11 March 2017